BIRD DOG MARKETING:

How to target true buyers and avoid making cold calls

W. Randy Murray

with contributors
Tony & Angie Ledford

The Bird Dog Marketing Program

W. Randy Murray
with contributors Tony & Angie Ledford

Published by Kennedy & Cohen Publishers
Clarksville, Georgia

706-886-0006

ISBN-13: 978-1508470120

ISBN-10: 150847102X

www.americaninsuranceinstitute.org

Book Design:

Pamela Adams Hirst

Albuquerque, NM

publishingpamela@yahoo.com

Acknowledgements

This book is a joint effort of written and verbal communication between myself, my associates and partners. In particular I want to mention Tony and Angie Ledford of Blue Ridge, Georgia. All my associates are my partners in this business as will you be, should you join our little family of agents and brokers across the United States. Some things will obviously be written by me and others not so obviously will be written or co-written between my partners and myself. Regardless of who writes what in this book, you can rest assured that we can teach anyone from A to Z how to properly execute our marketing programs.

What Do Others Say About
Randy Murray?

"Randy Murray is truly an Insurance Marketing Genius. In all the years I have been in this industry, I have never seen or been exposed to a greater marketing mind. Randy is the best at what he does, helping agents find and sell to people who want to buy life insurance. His methodologies and ideas are original and most importantly, very effective. Though people tried to copy Randy's work, there is and always will be only one Randy Murray."

— Brian Pope, President, Insurance Wholesalers

"Since 1988 when I met Randy Murray and was introduced to the Affordable Life Brochure, my income has not dropped below $250,000 annually. This may surprise some because I was diagnosed in 2001 with Muscular Dystrophy. Today, I am confined to a wheelchair but with access to a telephone and computer, my income has not suffered one penny."

— Ken Jones, President, Life Leads, Inc.

"I hold Randy Murray in the highest regard. He is a pioneer in the life insurance industry. I have never met anyone that has more knowledge about marketing life insurance and annuities than he does. If you want to become a success in our business, then follow the lead of Randy.

— Robert (Bob) C. Sosebee, President Emeritus,

First Standard Financial SBA Loan Originators

"Over the years, I have often referred to Randy Murray as an icon in the life insurance industry. Randy Murray, and the marketing system he designed, has single-handedly changed the way life insurance is marketed in the United States today! Oh, sure, I still see life insurance marketed in the traditional way. But then again, there is a blacksmith still doing business down the road from me.

"A man once asked me, 'If you wanted to teach your child to swim, to whom would you send that child, your neighbor who can't swim, or an Olympic swimmer?' If you want to make REAL money in the life insurance business, who are you going to listen to, your co-worker or the Icon? The choice is yours."

— Mike Hallmann former VP Marketing,

The Old Line Life Insurance Company of America

Dedication

We want to thank several people for contributing to this book. Many of the chapters in this book were written in large part by my brokers who are my family and friends. I do share authorship of this book with several, and they are: Ken Jones in Hartford, Connecticut; Eddie Emmett in Atlanta, Georgia; as well as Paul Himmelstein in Hartford, Connecticut.

THANK YOU, BRYAN POPE!

A special thanks to the man who saved my life, so to speak, when I came out of retirement. This man got me the companies and commission levels I needed to build another organization. His name is Bryan Pope and he is the owner of Insurance Wholesalers and Epic Marketing; both are a household name in our industry. I would not be back in business today had it not been for him. This man put an umbrella of protection over me that I needed, to keep away all the predators in this business that didn't want to see me as their competitor again. ...

THANK YOU, BRYAN POPE.

— Randy Murray

Table of Contents

BIRD DOG MARKETING:
How to target true buyers and avoid making cold calls

W. Randy Murray

with contributors
Tony & Angie Ledford

CHAPTER *One*

L ife is a series of opportunities. Even the ones we missed. This may be an opportunity or may not. That is up to you. One person in 1000 will see an ad about my program and respond ... they want information. They are looking for a better way, a better method of making a living. Of those 1000, one person in 40, or about 25–30, will actually join my little family each month. Of this number, approximately 5–6 will become "stars" of our business.

If this doesn't seem right to you, consider the fact that 9 in 10 people who enter the life insurance business will be gone completely, literally leave the business, in just two years or less. So this makes our numbers look unbelievably successful and it is looked upon by industry insiders as amazing. These 5–6 will change their lives for the better. These 5–6 will make more money than they had ever dreamed possible. These 5–6 will become part of and remain part of a small group of agents and brokers in the United States that have the most well-kept secret—how to put themselves in front of "buyers" of life insurance without having to cold call.

We will all fly away and leave this earth for hopefully a better place and when it is your time to make this journey, you can look back and say one of two things, "I did my best" or "I watched others do their best while I sat back doing nothing."

I know that I can say I did my best. I was able to provide for my family with a terrific standard of living all the while being a person who helped thousands. I will never look back on my life saying that I was sorry for what I have done. Sometimes I did great things like set up an endowment at the University of Georgia that provided scholarships for many students over the years who couldn't afford such an education. Sometimes I did things that would not be considered by some as significant, yet to me, they were great accomplishments. For instance, when I was a child in first grade, my family couldn't afford that box of Crayola Crayons, with 64 colors, all the colors of the rainbow. Only a few kids had parents who were able to spend the money to buy that box of crayons. So, when I had the money to spend, about 25 years ago, I started buying cases of Crayola Crayons in the 64-piece box and giving one box to all the kids in kindergarten and first grade at my home county's schools.

Every year for the past 25 years, every student received their box on the first day of school. I have seen some jump for joy, some actually start crying and some just sit in awe of the gift. It will make you start crying too if you just stand and watch them. This has expanded to all elementary schools in Northeast Georgia over the years. To me, this was a great thing but to others, perhaps not. I have never mentioned this crayon project to anyone, as I never mention to anyone anything I have ever done in a philanthropic way. This is something I prefer kept to myself, an opportunity to give back to my community is personal.

I am telling you all this because you have an opportunity to give your family and yourself a better standard of living and to have an opportunity to do great things for other people even if it's just giving a box of crayons to a child to brighten up his or her life for a day or two.

You can't do great things for others if you have no money to do so. Maybe it's time you changed your life. My program may not be the thing for you but you won't know until you read this book, so read on and give it a chance. Be one of those 5 or 6 who will become the

4

"stars," the ones who go on the insurance company conventions, the ones who stand up in the front of the room and get awards. Don't be the broker sitting in the back watching others receive all the accolades and praise. For one time in your life, be proud of yourself and look over to see the smile on the face of your wife when you reach out for her hand to walk with you to the front of the room to receive the reward for your efforts, that certificate or plaque for being the best. I did this for 16 straight years and it made everything worthwhile. The 14-hour days, and the sometimes 7-day work week. It made it all worth it.

After World War II, people had money to spend but very little to spend it on. Wartime industry had not yet converted to peacetime industry and people wanted things and couldn't buy them.

My father opened a small 12' x 12' store in our little town of Toccoa, Georgia, on Main Street. He sold a little furniture, mostly appliances small and large.

Every Monday, he would get in his truck with a small trailer and head out to Atlanta to call on manufacturers and distributors. Since supply was very limited, he literally had to beg this one for a couple of toasters, the next one for a mixer or two, then the big job of getting a refrigerator or washing machine out of another.

By the end of the day, he had filled up his truck and trailer with merchandise, headed home and spent most of the evening stocking his shelves. He did this by himself. He had no help. During the week he would sell most, but not all of the things he had purchased that past Monday.

On Saturday evening, he would close and come home to take my mom, my brother and me to a "fish house" located out in the county. We would eat and he would go table to table introducing himself and trying to set up sales for the next week.

On Sunday, we would all get up, get dressed and go to church. After Sunday services we would go home where Mom would cook her usual pot roast and we were lucky to have that. Dad would take a nap and then around 2:00, he would get up and do the strangest thing. He would take our Sunday paper, divide it up then wrap it around his legs. He would attach that newspaper to his legs with large sturdy rubber bands and then put either me or my brother up in the truck with him and head for his store.

Dad would load everything in the store and I mean everything that he hadn't sold the previous week into the truck and head out into the rural areas of North Georgia.

He would proceed to pick out a dirt road to target and stop at every country house he came to. He would get out of his truck leaving me and my brother sitting in the cab and walk up to the house. More often than not, here came the dogs. Everyone in those days had pretty mean dogs in their yard. Many times these dogs would attack him. I don't mean bark at him, I mean jump on him. Often they would latch onto his legs chewing away with the most awful growling sounds.

This never stopped him. He walked right up to that house. If he didn't get an answer at the front door, he would go to the back. Then he'd take off his hat and say, "I'm Clyde Murray and I own Deluxe Tire and Appliance in Toccoa. I just stopped by to see if there were any household items you good folks may want or need today. I have some supplies right there on my truck and I sure would appreciate an opportunity to show them to you."

Was he successful? Well, in 1965 our whole family, and by then there were six of us, went to New York to the Waldorf Astoria Hotel where Dad got the award for being the number-one retailer of General Electric appliances in the United States.

Now, I am telling you this story to say, maybe I do have a jump on you. And maybe, just maybe I don't have the call reluctance you probably have. Maybe I can do our program better than you but what does it matter? I am going to teach you how to do it and when you finish reading this book, you will know as much about it as I do. So, read on.

REMEMBER:

Don't be frightened that your life may change after reading this. Put aside, even if just for an hour, your feelings that someone is trying to cheat you. Just because you have bought leads or lead systems in the past that didn't work out just as you had hoped, this isn't one of them. I am not charging you a thousand dollars for this information I am giving it to you, so leave your feelings of doubt behind and read on.

CHAPTER Two

An Introduction to the Famous
"BIRD DOG" Program

Eli Lilly develops a new drug. They send their salesmen out to sell it. Who do they call on? Right, they call the doctors. However, the doctors don't sell the drug. Who does? Right! They send the patients to the pharmacy. The pharmacy actually sells the drug. Ely Lilly makes it, the pharmacy sells it, but neither would make or sell it if it weren't for the doctor, who I like to call the facilitator or in street lingo, the "bird dog."

Chevron manufactures gasoline and they send their salesmen out to sell it. Who do they call on? They do not call on the gas stations. Rather the gas and oil distributors. You know who they are. Every town of any size in America has one. In my home town it's Acree Oil Company.

So Chevron, the manufacturer and your local gas station—the retailer, would not survive if it were not for the distributor or who I refer to again as the facilitator or the "bird dog."

They say that there are up to 8000 items in the typical full-service grocery store. There are thousands of companies that produce these products. They send their salesmen to sell their products and who do they call on? It surely isn't the grocery stores because if there were thousands of salesmen calling on every single grocery store, the customers couldn't get in the doors. They sell to a grocery wholesaler or in the trade known as a grocery distributor. The manufacturers make said product. The grocery store sells the product. Neither would survive if it were not for the middle man—the facilitator, as I call him, the "bird dog."

Two thirds of all goods and services in the United States and probably in the world would not be made or sold if it were not for some type of middle man, some type of facilitator or "bird dog." It's a fact but I think that most businessmen have never really looked at it quite this way. Our economy is based on whether or not these "bird dogs" survive and do their job properly.

What I have done over the past twenty years is help identify and set up strategic relationships with facilitators or again as I like to call them "bird dogs" for the life insurance industry. The same thing has been done for almost every other industry in this country but for some unknown reason, no one seems to have accomplished this for the life insurance business. One quick note to mention, the material in this book can be used by any person in almost any industry. The principles are the same. So, if you are not in life insurance or related lines, don't worry. Keep reading. Chances are what I will be teaching you will also apply to what you do. So, remember, all I have done is help life insurance agents to FIND PEOPLE WHO WILL SEND YOU INDIVIDUALS WHO HAVE SAID, "I WANT TO BUY LIFE INSURANCE." I HAVE DEVELOPED A LEAD GENERATION SYSTEM THAT COSTS NEXT TO NOTHING TO EXECUTE. KEEP READING. I KNOW MANY OF YOU DON'T BELIEVE WHAT I AM SAYING RIGHT NOW BUT IT IS THE TRUTH.

We all know that life insurance agents have been encouraged over the years to establish a relationship with an independent property and casualty insurance agency. Just to convince them to allow you to work their files so to speak and you split the commissions on all policies you sell to their customers. Sounds great, but I have yet to know one agent in my 41-year career who ever did this and sold the first policy. The reason, well there are many but primarily the owners of the independent property and casualty insurance agencies really do not want you messing around in their files and let you know that from the beginning and then don't cooperate with you like they should to make your relationship work. So, what I did was rework the plan and find a different way to make that relationship work. And it does work! I simply found a way to approach an independent property and casualty insurance agency more commonly known as an auto and homeowner agency. You know the agency we see when we drive down the main street of almost any town. Most are independently owned and operated. Most are still run by the person who started the agency many years ago or one of their family members. Most are quite successful and profitable.

You have to know that most independent property and casualty insurance agency owners do not need you. They will set up a relationship with you but only if you approach them properly.

Independent property and casualty insurance agencies are only one of a number of "bird dogs" where a strategic relationship can be established by a life insurance broker, but it is one of the best. For decades I have based my business on establishing "bird dog" relationships and made millions while helping others to also make millions. One of the principles we will mention later on in this book that you should remember—being a good salesman, has absolutely nothing to do with being successful in our business. We are all good salesmen. I've heard over one hundred times, "That boy could sell ice to an Eskimo. I just can't understand why he isn't very successful."

WELL, LET ME TELL YOU—THE SECRET TO BEING A SUCCESSFUL SALESPERSON IS GETTING IN FRONT OF PEOPLE WHO WANT TO BUY LIFE INSURANCE, AND IN TURN, SELLING THEM YOUR PRODUCT.

To carry this a bit further, when you buy an ad in your local newspaper to advertise life or health insurance the newspaper is in a round-about way the facilitator. The life insurance company develops the products, and you in turn sell the products. If running an ad worked properly in your local paper, then the newspaper would be that facilitator or "bird dog." The newspaper would be the impetus behind the development and sale of a policy to someone. The problem with this analogy is that newspaper advertising isn't free. It is expensive and most life insurance agents either cannot afford to spend the money to advertise or their wife won't let them gamble that money not knowing whether it will generate any sales at all. I don't mean this as a joke. Most life insurance agents are men and most of them have the family purse strings controlled by their wife. In my career I have found very few of these wives who would gamble a few dollars on the family business without some guarantee of the outcome. We all know there are no guarantees in our business or life in general. This is the biggest reason most men settle for a life of mediocrity or failure. If this sounds sexist, then so be it, but it is the truth.

So, why is advertising not the strategic relationship we are looking for? Because it costs money to advertise and if "bird dog" relationships are set up properly, the way I am going to teach you in this short book it costs almost nothing to do it properly. What you are really doing is setting up relationships that work on the old "I will scratch your back if you will scratch my back" theory and it does work and has worked for me for decades. I did advertise over the years but not in traditional ways and when I did advertise, I knew that my advertising would work and was not a gamble. So when I advertised it was more of a "bird dog" type relationship that is impossible for most of you reading this to accomplish.

Over the years, I have run ads in association magazines— publications that hit specific special interest groups such as—The National Association of Farmers or The National Association of Nurses, etc. There are over 300,000 of them in the United States and growing by approximately 6000 each year. You run a small ad and the members who receive the magazine think that the association has endorsed you. I can't control the perception but it sure helps. The members who receive these magazines, in turn, respond to the advertisement. They call you and buy life insurance. The best part— there is almost never another insurance agent or company that advertises in these publications. You are the only one. You have it all to yourself and to carry it a step further—no life insurance agent has ever advertised in that magazine.

We once ran a 2" ad in the *Blood Horse Breeders Association* magazine that resulted in the sale of 9 new policies of $1,000,000 or more in face amount. The gross commission from this one publication was in excess of $50,000. This is from running just one ad, one time. This does not happen every day, but it does happen.

We found that specific special interest publications about horses, skeet shooting, and polo really appealed to people with higher incomes. Golf and tennis, which would be the first inclination of some agents wanting to advertise, did not work. We do not know why these ads did not work, we just found out after losing our money running several in golf/tennis publications. Why did LPN association magazines work and RN not work? No one knows for sure.

Why did trial lawyer association magazines work and corporate lawyer magazines not? Again, it's unknown, but we analyzed our responses and in turn focused our advertising on publications that did work and forgot the rest.

This is one of thousands of things I learned searching for facilitators or "bird dogs" over the years. Trial and error was my game for some two decades. I bet I wasted five million dollars during the 1990's alone just testing things that didn't work.

I once placed 60,000 brochures in *Southern Living* magazine at a cost of $35,000, only to realize that I had inadvertently left my address off of the return card. I once inserted 300,000 pieces into the Orange County Register newspaper in California and forgot to put my phone number on the insert.

I learned many lessons and the primary beneficiary of my mistakes today are the brokers who associate themselves with me and my agency. These brokers are now the winners because of what I have learned, the beneficiaries of my trial and error tactics.

ASSOCIATION PUBLICATION ADVERTISING DOES WORK IF YOU KNOW WHAT YOU ARE DOING. LET ME ASSURE YOU, AT THIS STAGE, YOU DO NOT KNOW WHAT YOU ARE DOING, AND IT WOULD BE A WASTE OF YOUR MONEY.

DID YOU KNOW THAT IF YOU RUN YOUR AD ON THE RIGHT HAND PAGE, IT DOUBLES THE NUMBER OF RESPONSES VERSUS RUNNING IT ON THE LEFT HAND PAGE? DID YOU KNOW THAT RUNNING AN AD IN THE TOP, RIGHT-HAND CORNER OF A PAGE WILL TRIPLE YOUR RESPONSE RATHER THAN IF YOU RAN THAT SAME AD IN THE BOTTOM LEFT HAND CORNER? IF YOU RUN AN AD ON THE FIRST 7 PAGES OF THE MAGAZINE ON EVERY OTHER ODD NUMBER PAGE, 1, 3, 5, 7, 9, 11 OR 13, YOUR RESPONSE WILL ALSO DOUBLE VERSUS IF YOU RUN YOUR AD ON ANY OTHER PAGE IN THE BOOK. DID YOU KNOW THAT IF YOU RUN AN AD IN A MAGAZINE WITH LESS THAN 30 PAGES YOU CAN INCREASE YOUR RESULTS UP TO FOUR TIMES THAN IF THE MAGAZINE IS OVER 30 PAGES LONG? I COULD GO ON AND ON BUT THE REASON YOU WON'T BE SUCCESSFUL AT THIS STAGE IS BECAUSE YOU DON'T KNOW THESE INTIMATE DETAILS.

What you will be reading over the next few pages is not a novel. It is not an extensive article. It is a summary of the most important points that make the "bird dog" program work.

What I can say can be said in a few pages. They said that Sylvester Stallone wrote the book/movie "Rocky" in just two days and it took him to riches. Well, this certainly isn't "Rocky" but it doesn't take months to write what I am going to write because I have lived what I'm writing. I know this stuff like the back of my hand.

Have you ever read a diet book? You know, the *Atkins Diet* or something like that. In the 200 pages or so, you will find a few pages that describe the diet, and the bulk of the remaining pages talk about nothing.

They are called fillers. I am not singling out this one book. Most diet books are the same way—one or two pages on the diet and the other pages on exercise, foods, attitude, etc.

I am eliminating the filler pages and the unnecessary information and getting right to how my program works. By the way, I do not use the word "system" because I believe that anything that carries the word "system" in the title, you should run away from, all the while holding your wallet. The reason I am telling you this is because I don't want you to think that a shorter book means it's any less informative or less truthful.

When I give a seminar to my agency field forces in different cities, a very small percentage actually take what I teach them and do anything with it. I would venture to say that if 50 agents are in a room, maybe 5 actually leave that room and make money—big money—with what I teach them. They all should. What I have learned can be mastered by a ten-year-old in a couple of hours. If you are one who will do something with it, then I am at your disposal. If you are not one of the players in our business who has that "fire in your belly," so to speak, yearning for a better life, then don't bother me, because I spend my time with winners. Why doesn't everyone take my teaching and become successful with it? Many reasons. Some are lazy and have no ambition. They think they are smarter than I am, and they may very well be, but not when it comes to my lead program. Some want to change what I teach them and do things their way. They try to find a short cut and there are no short cuts. Another reason is reluctance. They have been knocked down so much in their careers, in their lives, which makes them give up. What they don't realize is how drastically their lives can be changed by just forgetting the past for one day, just one day. Do what I instruct through this book and they will wake up for the first time in their career with someone to talk to, more importantly, somewhere to go that day.

In sales, we wake up every single day of our lives unemployed. Unless we sell something that day, or any day, regardless of how many calls are made, regardless of how many letters are typed, regardless of how many conversations are held with others, if nothing is sold, no money is made. Isn't that one heck of a way to live? If your friends, or especially your family really knew what you mentally have to go through, almost every single day of your life, THEY WOULD BE SHOCKED. You get out of bed, knowing that if you don't sell something that day, usually to someone you have never met, you will not have the money to buy food or put a roof over your family's head. It is one terrible mental affliction all salesmen go through in their lives. If our families knew what we have to go through, maybe they would be a little more understanding. OK, now let's get down to it. Start reading and remember what you read. Read these next few pages a dozen times before you go to bed tonight.

Memorize all you can. And yes, I say—memorize. Some of it requires memorization or you will stumble and not be successful. Stand in front of your mirror in the morning and practice what you are going to say that day.

Forget the past. Forget all the people who have dragged you down in your business and life in general. Pick yourself up, go to work, and don't be afraid of anyone. If someone is rude to you, turn around, walk away and forget it. I am serious.

REMEMBER:

Don't let anyone grab your self-respect and get away with it. Not ever again. Stand up for yourself. Get mad and go get 'em. Life isn't fair, and in these economic times, you cannot be the nice guy and win.

CHAPTER Three

The Affordable Life Brochure

You will be reading throughout this book about the Affordable Life Brochure being king. The brochure is the key to everything. Without the brochure, you are wasting your time if you even start practicing my marketing programs.

I developed the Affordable Life Brochure after years of work. Trial and error is an understatement when talking about this marketing piece. It literally took five years of day and night tweaking to get something that people would pick up, read and then call to buy life insurance from me.

However, I finally did get something to work, and boy, oh boy, did it ever work. Between 1990 and 1999 over one million policies were sold as a direct result of this brochure. A direct result of people seeing the marketing piece, looking it over, and then taking action by either calling my office or filling out a return card and mailing it to me.

Can you really grasp one million policies? Let me tell you, IT IS MORE THAN 99% OF WHAT ALL LIFE INSURANCE COMPANIES HAVE IN FORCE TODAY.

Peace
of Mind
for a more secure
tomorrow.

American Insurance Institute
Box M
Toccoa, Georgia
30577

706-968-5584

Bird Dog Marketing
Box M
Toccoa, Georgia 30577

BUSINESS REPLY MAIL
FIRST-CLASS MAIL PERMIT NO.
POSTAGE WILL BE PAID BY ADDRESSEE

American Insurance Institute
Box M
Toccoa, Georgia
30577

LOOK AT MY MARKETING BROCHURE ONCE MORE.
YOUR NAME COULD BE ON THIS BROCHURE TOO!

Importance Of The Affordable Life Brochure

The previous two pages of this book shows a copy of one of my famous brochures. It is not complicated. It is not difficult to understand. I can still remember waking my wife at two in the morning one night in 1979. I was quite excited. I said "Honey, I have finally figured out what was missing from my brochure!" It should be PINK. "Why?" she asked. "Well, since I think mostly women send the return card in or make the call to buy insurance—and women prefer the color pink to other colors."

HOW STUPID I WAS. I kept trying and coming up with ideas, until finally in 1985, I made it work and here is what happened. Read carefully. This is a true story.

It was the fall of 1985. I had sold pretty much everything. My family—my wife and two small children—was sleeping on cots. Our pantry inventory was down to a few canned goods. I had spent it all. I had sold or hocked everything. I had run up the credit cards and borrowed all that I could. It was almost over. I had spent it all experimenting with my brochure and my marketing theories. As crazy as this may sound, I really did. I knew my ideas would work. I knew that people would pick up their phones, call a life insurance agent and buy—all over the phone. I just knew it, and I would do anything to prove it and almost had.

Life and health insurance companies would supply agents with all the ad slicks they wanted to run in a newspaper. The only problem was, none of them worked. They were sure pretty, but THEY JUST DID NOT WORK.

Time Insurance Company in Milwaukee, Wisconsin, was the foremost individual major medical company in the business. They had beautiful, and what was thought to be effective, advertisements we could use in our local papers or on our local radio stations. I spent money over a period of years, running these ads and never selling the first policy. By now, you should know me well enough to know that I didn't quit. Apparently a mule has to kick me in the head to get me to abandon anything that has to do with marketing or testing marketing ideas.

The only item of value I had left was a 1982 Buick Riviera. I went to the bank and borrowed $3000 against this car. I took that money and bought $100 worth of groceries. Next, I sent a $2,850 check to the *Gwinnette Daily News* in Duluth, Georgia, to distribute and print 50,000 of my brochures for that next week. With the remaining $50, I went to a local pawn shop and bought a "Saturday night special" .38 pistol and they threw in 2 bullets. I fully intended to use that gun on myself if that distribution, or as we called it, that "drop," did not work well that next week. I had no choice. I was broke and didn't expect anyone to help me, not friends, nor family. My father was a millionaire but that man wouldn't give me or my children, his own grandchildren, a sandwich if we were hungry. I think it was because he had lived through the Great Depression. From that, he had learned how important money was.

I had a wife and two small children who had no food, and soon, no roof over their heads if my final marketing experiment didn't work. I had life insurance and knew that they could live decently with a home and food, and one day, an education if they got my insurance money, and I would not deny them this just because their father was "nuts," and believe me, I thought I was, sometimes. Today, it infuriates me when an agent says—well, I put out 500 of your brochures in our local grocery store flyer and haven't had a single call yet. Your program stinks. I quit! Can you imagine if I had quit? All the work I put in to making this program work and this guy had spent less than a hundred bucks and was ready to throw in the towel? It is not uncommon to hear agents say similar things to me. It's just, today I don't hate them like I once did.

Today, I pity them. (If I would listen to my friend George Litchfield, I would be praying for them.) I really feel sorry for them because I know they and their families are destined to live a life of mediocrity, at best, and that is a real shame when they could live so much better. Their kids could get a superior education.

They could live in much nicer homes. They could be more active in their communities and help people. What a shame!

For several years prior to this time, I had only advertised with my brochure in newspapers in the North Georgia mountain counties, never in a big-city paper, and I thought, what the heck, why not go out with a big bang. So, I took my last brochures and stuck them in a big-city paper. If I was going to shoot myself for failure, at least, maybe this way, people would remember me.

The "Affordable Life Brochures" went out on Wednesday of the next week. I didn't like Thursdays because my brochure got "lost" in the grocery store ads that came out weekly on Thursdays and Fridays. I couldn't sleep that night. I paced the floors. At six that morning, I took a shower and went into my kids' room and just sat there for a few minutes looking at them and I said a prayer that they would be alright without a dad. I kissed them both and went to the office. At 7:26 a.m., I remember that time very vividly, it was an Eastern Airlines pilot calling me on the phone. He had read my brochure in the paper while having breakfast at the Waffle House near highway I-85 and Druid Hills Road in Atlanta. He was calling to say he wanted to buy a $250,000 life insurance policy and asked would it be alright if he drove up to my office, 105 miles away, to fill out the application. I am not lying. Not only did this absolutely knock me out of my chair, since I had never written a policy of this size, but by the time he got to my office, I had also received a half dozen more calls, all buyers. The next day, my post office box was full of return cards from people wanting to buy.

These were not leads, rather actual people that had chosen a face amount, seen the premium cost, and wanted to buy.

I never looked back. I went on to build a multi-million dollar agency. In 1989, I started teaching my program to other agents across the United States. By 1999, we had sold, as best I could calculate,

1,223,556 life insurance policies using my advertising piece and my marketing programs. What a great life I have had. More than 13,000 agents contracted with me during that time and we would fill up cruise ships and hotels every year with agents on our annual conventions. In 1996, I rented the Ectas, the entire ship, on her maiden voyage, filled with over 1000 of my brokers and their spouses, for a full week. What a great time we had! Some of the greatest things about being successful were the trips. Every trip was another adventure.

Why do my brochure and my marketing programs work so well? It is because we tell people what they want to know and hear before making that buying decision and they are:

1. What we sell (Life Insurance).

2. What it costs.

3. Who we are.

4. How to contact us if they want to buy.

That's it. That is all we say on our brochure. That is all we tell them. Insurance companies like Prudential own a piece of the rock; Allstate puts you in good hands. These are just two of dozens of companies that want brand advertising, with their company slogan only. It is great to get people to know who they are, but does absolutely nothing for an agent. Ask a Prudential agent how many phone calls or insurance sales he has made when the client says they decided to "buy a piece of the rock." They will tell you, never.

Our marketing programs using our Affordable Life Brochures work well for insurance agents and brokers. What we do isn't rocket science, and after you finish reading, you will say to yourself, "This is so easy, it couldn't work." You may also say, "There is no way this Murray guy invented this thing. It is too simple." Well, I did and it does. Read on.

One last thing. Regardless of what you say or think, you do have call reluctance. If you didn't, you would not be reading this book.

Many of these motivational gurus we see on television in commercials have built mini-empires on telling you, the problem is, you are afraid to make a sale, and then they proclaim to have a solution for this problem. I have never heard more hogwash in my life.

Call reluctance is caused by a fear of people, not a fear of making a sale. All of us have had bad experiences in our sales careers. When you are asked about your most memorable sale, most of you will not tell a story about a big sale, rather the big one that you didn't make, and usually because you were trying to sell a policy to some rude "horse's ass." You have call reluctance because you don't want to relive this experience, and rightfully so.

REMEMBER:

I will mention this again in this book, on more than one occasion, but don't think you are the only person who has ever been treated badly. The key is being able to put it out of your mind or YOU WON'T BE SUCCESSFUL WITH MY PROGRAM, OR ANY PROGRAM FOR THAT MATTER.

CHAPTER Four

Marketing

In 1969, there was a contest within the marketing departments of most colleges and universities in the United States and Western Europe. The winner would be the student who came up with the best definition of marketing. They wanted a definition that could be published in marketing textbooks in the future. I won the contest and my marketing definition is still in textbooks at universities such as Harvard and Oxford. This is probably the only contest I ever entered and won, but what an honor it is for me to read my definition in major college textbooks.

Marketing is the total system of interacting business activities designed to do four things—plan, price, promote and sell any product or service to present or potential customers.

This is the only accurate definition of marketing you will ever read. Let's just take a minute and tear this apart. Marketing, that is what we do. We are marketers. We are not inventors of anything, we just market, or shall I say, everyone reading this does a form of marketing and that is sales. Read the definition again. Marketing is made up of four parts—planning, pricing the product, promoting or advertising in some way, and the actual sale. You are the one making the sale and completing the marketing process.

The life insurance companies are the manufacturers of a life insurance product. Their product people, sometimes along with their marketing people, design a product. Very little of this is inventive. Most of this is just copying other insurance companies' work. They also price their product.

This is done by the actuaries. They take the actuarial tables and determine how many people are going to die within a certain period of time. They build in company expenses, commissions, salaries, marketing and even down to the cost of an annual convention. The insurance company designs and prices the products you sell.

That is their job, planning and pricing the product. It is not their job to promote or sell the product. Stop blaming them if you can't find someone to sell to tomorrow.

Then comes the promotion and sale of the products and this is where the rub comes in. Insurance companies don't know how to promote, and advertise to find new clients for you, so they give that responsibility to you.

You are responsible for selling the product. I have met very few agents in my life who could promote themselves and their products and additionally to consistently put themselves in front of people who want to buy what they sell. They could sell but not promote or do what was necessary to find new clients commonly called prospects.

Promotion isn't your responsibility. It is the responsibility of the insurance company to plan and price products. It is your responsibility to sell the products. But the responsibility for promoting the products or getting you in front of potential clients (if you can't do it and most of you reading this can't or you wouldn't be reading this book) is the responsibility of the field marketing organization (FMO) you are associated with. If the insurance company can't do it and you can't do it, which most agents can't, then it is the FMO that must do it or you will have thousands of licensed agents running all over the place doing basically nothing but talking on the phone and selling nothing.

If you are an agent/broker and you are working under an FMO, and not directly with a company, then it is the responsibility of that FMO to do the promotion. It is their responsibility to justify the override they are making.

Their number-one responsibility is promoting the product, putting you in front of people who want to buy life insurance. This is not your responsibility as an insurance professional. You sell the insurance, the company designs and prices it, and the FMO should promote it. The problem: most FMOs DO NOT PROMOTE BECAUSE THEY DON'T KNOW HOW. THEY GIVE YOU A CONTRACT AND SAY, "GO GET 'EM." YOU ARE SUPPOSED TO FIND SOMEONE TO SELL.

Most FMOs have thousands of brokers and they hope each one sells 2 to 3 policies per year. If you multiply 2 or 3 times 1000 agents/brokers, they can easily make millions while you starve. In our business it is time for these giant FMOs to begin earning their money and do something for their agents/brokers. The worst thing is, the money that an insurance company dedicates to a marketing company never gets to the agent who is actually selling the product. That money for promoting that life insurance company's products is utterly wasted. If an insurance company would ever look and see how many agents under contract ever actually make a sale, it would shock them. If no one truly knows how to put an agent in front of a prospect to make a sale, how can they be expected to sell anything? The insurance company does not know how to promote; the FMO does not know how to promote. This explains the 90% attrition rate in our industry. Within three years, 9 out of 10 people who choose life insurance sales as a career are gone.

Stop feeling bad. Stop thinking you are doing something wrong because you have great difficulty finding new clients. It is not your job, nor has it ever been, but when neither company nor FMO can promote, this responsibility gets dumped on you.

Now, how to solve this promotion problem. You either associate yourself with an FMO that does know how, or you associate yourself with an FMO that will teach you how to generate your own new clients. There are not many, but there are some. I can do it. Andy Albright of National Agents Alliance (NAA) can do it. There are indeed others, but it's difficult to find them.

Twenty-five years ago, I developed, through a hell of a lot of work, while spending every cent my family had, a lead program that worked. I learned how to promote the sale of life insurance, and since that time, I have been personally doing this program and teaching others how to do it themselves.

REMEMBER:

IT IS NOT, AND NEVER HAS BEEN, YOUR RESPONSIBILITY TO PROMOTE THE SALE OF LIFE INSURANCE. IT HAS BEEN THE RESPONSIBILITY OF YOUR FMO. UNFORTUNATELY, EVEN THOUGH IT IS THEIR RESPONSIBILITY TO HELP YOU FIND NEW CLIENTS, THEY DO NOT KNOW HOW. IT IS NOT THE FAULT OF THE INSURANCE COMPANY, SO STOP BLAMING THEM. IT IS THE RESPONSIBILITY OF THE PERSON YOU HAVE CONTRACTED WITH, THE PERSON WHO MAKES AN OVERRIDE ON YOU, THE FMO. WHEN THE DAY COMES THAT THE INSURANCE COMPANIES START GETTING SOME OF THEIR MARKETING FUNDS DIRECTLY INTO THE HANDS OF THE FMOs THAT KNOW HOW TO PROMOTE, THEN THIS INDUSTRY WILL CHANGE FOR THE BETTER.

YOU ARE READING THIS BOOK, WRITTEN AND DEVELOPED BY ME, W. RANDY MURRAY, AND SOME OF MY ASSOCIATES, BECAUSE YOU HAVE COME TO ME TO HELP YOU DEVELOP NEW CLIENTS AND TO TEACH YOU HOW TO DO IT YOURSELF. THIS BOOK IS NOT MEANT FOR OTHERS. IT IS ONLY MEANT FOR BROKERS WHO HAVE ASSOCIATED THEMSELVES WITH ME, RANDY MURRAY. MY MARKETING MATERIALS, MY AFFORDABLE LIFE BROCHURE AND ITS ACCOMPANYING MARKETING AND

PROMOTION PROGRAM ARE PROPRIETARY INFORMATION. I DEVELOPED THEM AND I HAVE COPYRIGHTED THEM. IF YOU COPY THIS BOOKLET OR COPY WHAT IS IN IT, YOU WILL BE IN COURT VERY SOON. FOR THOSE OF YOU READING THIS WHO ARE ETHICAL AND HONEST PEOPLE, READ ON AND YOU WILL BE SO EXCITED WHEN YOU FINISH, YOU WILL NOT BE ABLE TO SLEEP TONIGHT. I PROMISE.

CHAPTER Five

Key States

Insurance is sold in all 50 states. There are some states that are more lucrative. In order, they are:

1. California

2. Texas

3. Florida

4. Pennsylvania

5. Illinois

6. New Jersey

7. Arizona

8. North Carolina

9. Virginia

10. Maryland

11. Massachusetts

12. Connecticut

13. Ohio

Additionally, there are ten cities, none of which are in the 13 great states. These were our top producing cities for many years:

1. Las Vegas, Nevada*
2. Charleston, South Carolina
3. Portland, Oregon
4. Baton Rouge, Louisiana
5. Phoenix, Arizona
6. Detroit, Michigan*
7. Augusta, Georgia
8. Salt Lake City, Utah
9. Portland, Maine
10. Dover, Delaware

* I would think that Las Vegas and Detroit would no longer fit into the category of top ten, but all cities in this country are good if you have the guts to get out of your chair and go to work.

Watch out for something. If you are shopping around for a company or FMO to work with, look on the wall in the executive's office. If he has a pin (you know, one of those red plastic type pins) and he has one proudly stuck in each state, then start running. It means his ego, not his best sense, is at work. It is more important for him to tell you he has representation in an area, even if it's not a productive region, than it is for him to tell you that he is well represented in the better areas. What he is telling you is that they spend their marketing money, 60% of it, in areas that do you no good. So, if you need help in the marketing side, or if you need some funds, you won't get it from this man or woman.

CHAPTER Six

Lead Programs

Most lead programs are not less effective than they have been in the past, they just don't work well to start with. I could give you a long list of lead programs, most of which we all have been taught in the past. Most of these are from people who don't have a clue as to what they are talking about when it comes to prospecting for clients, but as I said, I am not here to write a lengthy book. What I am saying is true.

Throw out everything you have ever been taught about prospecting for new life insurance clients and start fresh today. I entered the life insurance business while a senior at the University of Georgia in 1969. All I did was knock on doors, every door. I was just 19 years old. What a way to begin.

I would find a street in a busy area. I would drive my car one mile from a gas station or a fast food restaurant, then cross over and drive back. I would park at that gas station because, usually, they would not tow you away, if you asked. I would get my little briefcase (everyone had a briefcase in those days) and start walking. I would stop at every house, business, farm—it didn't matter—but I never missed one place or person. One of the largest sales I made was to a farmer plowing his field. I could see him from the road. I climbed over a barbed-wire fence and just walked up to him. I still don't know if I was more afraid of him, or he of me. He stopped plowing, we greeted each other, and he invited me to his house for a glass of iced tea. I climbed up on the fender of the tractor and off we went to the house. To make a long story short, I ended up writing the man a nice whole life policy and one on his wife. (In those days, term life insurance didn't readily exist. The only term I had ever seen was a level term to age 65, but it cost basically the same as a whole life policy.) I remember it as if it were yesterday. The total monthly premium was a little over $200 and my commission was half that. In those days, commissions were nowhere near what you can get today. Now, $1,200 doesn't sound like a great deal today but that was the equivalent of almost three months' salary in 1969. That ended up being my largest sale for the year and I thought I had made a million dollars. I went on to graduate, and instead of pursuing my life insurance sales career, I took a job at $490 a month, selling detergent to grocery stores for Procter and Gamble. My father told me that he hadn't wasted his money on my education for me to end up peddling life insurance to strangers. "Anyone can do that," he would say.

"I will be ashamed if you don't get a legitimate job," he would say. I was devastated, but I took that job, and for a year, I became accustomed to a standard of living that couldn't be sustained on that small income. Another year was spent with a major company, Libbey Glass, and I couldn't take the minimal salary any longer. I moved back to Athens, Georgia, went back into the life insurance business, and have never looked back. Over the next ten years, I sold, much of it by continuing to knock on doors, trying almost every prospecting program I was told worked. I would read what agents would write, telling people their system worked, but mostly, I just invented methods of getting customers without having to knock on doors. I don't know why I wanted to quit what I was doing, but I guess everyone wants a better way.

Remember how we were told to make a list of 100 friends, family, neighbors, associates and co-workers, anyone we knew or thought we knew, call on them and sell them life insurance? That went over like someone passing gas in church. I still remember going to my cousin's house for a family reunion one bright sunny Sunday afternoon. Within fifteen minutes of my arrival, everyone had migrated as far away as they could from me for fear I would try to sell them life insurance. I don't think it could have been any worse.

I still remember what I thought was a brilliant idea. I would put together sales materials, and call on pastors of area churches. I would try to convince them to let me sell their members a life insurance policy and leave the benefits to the church. It sounded terrific, and I had my first church ready to go, but the pastor felt we should talk to the board of deacons. I made the presentation, and all but one thought it was a terrific idea. That one was a State Farm agent who promptly stood up and said, "Why would we go to an outsider? I like the idea but I can do this." All involved promptly agreed and that was the end of my church lead program.

Payroll deduction market sounded good after reading an article in *Life Insurance Selling* magazine. I sold a local junior college on letting me make a presentation that next month to all their employees. The meeting was almost over. I was standing in the hall waiting on my time to talk. The dean of the school opened the door and invited me in. The crowd seemed a little intimidating, but I knew what I was going to say in my fifteen minutes. I was determined no one was going to frighten me off.

The dean addressed the employees, "This is Randy Murray. He is a life insurance salesman. He is here today to sell life insurance to anyone that is interested." He then said, "If you want to buy some life insurance, you can stay, if you are not interested, you may go." Well, I am sure glad I wasn't standing in the way of the door, because I would have been trampled by the bunch, running like I had leprosy. That was the end of my payroll deduction career.

I could go on and on, but I won't. The point is—do what I did. Find something that does work for you and stick with it. Repetition of a skill is what successful people are doing every day. Do you think an actor gets up on the stage every night and ad-libs his dialogue? He doesn't.

37

He says the same thing over and over. This is how successful actors are made. We should do the same.

So, I am telling you that what I do works. If you learn it, you should do it every day for the rest of your sales career. It's important to keep doing whatever it is you do now until you learn my "bird dog" program and gradually work in this new method of prospecting. DO NOT QUIT WHAT YOU ARE DOING NOW. SLOWLY LEARN AND IMPLEMENT OUR MARKETING PROGRAM.

Tomorrow morning, it is your job to start establishing relationships with new people who will send you other new people who want to buy life insurance. I am not talking about their friends or neighbors who might want to consider buying life insurance one day. I am saying that you are to start developing relationships with people who will send you people who want to buy life insurance, people who will say, "Yes, I want to buy some life insurance. Whom do I go see?" Impossible, you say, to find such a person?

Well, I have found, directly or through brokers who have worked with me, over 1,200,000 people who have purchased life insurance from me since the beginning of the 1990's. Yes, that is right! Thousands of people have sent my agency over one-million-two-hundred-thousand other people who did buy life insurance, health insurance, pension plans, annuities, and just about every other form of insurance that exists. Amazing isn't it?

A "bird dog" is a person who will send to you other people who will buy life insurance from you. From this day on, it is your job to find and set up relationships with "bird dogs."

Here is a list of the top 10 "bird dogs":

1. Health Insurance Agents

2. Residential Mortgage Brokers

3. Property and Casualty Insurance Agencies

4. Bookkeepers and CPAs

5. Tax Preparation Services

6. Savings & Loan and Bank Loan Officers

7. Small Business Administration (SBA) Loan Originators

8. Stockbrokers

9. Real Estate Agencies

10. ...and Anyone Else In the World

Anyone can be a "bird dog." This is simply a list of 9 distinct groups of individuals who work best. This group of individuals will send other people to you who will buy life insurance from you when you approach them correctly. Approach and service make a successful "bird dog." Let me show you what I mean.

What are we trying to get these people and organizations to do? If you will send us people who want to buy life insurance, then we will either pay you a commission/finder's fee or we will send you people who buy your services or products, or a combination of the two. You scratch my back and I will scratch yours. What you want is to set up a relationship, or in new economic terms, a strategic relationship with someone else that will benefit you both. In our language, a "bird dog" is simply a relationship.

Bird dogs hunt. You are looking for people who will hunt for you— people who will hunt for other people who want to buy life insurance.

We all have heard of, or participated in, things like "Business after Hours" programs. Many of them are sponsored by local Chambers of Commerce across the country. They are designed to help you find a bird dog or two in nice surroundings. The problem with these is that, once you leave the gathering, no one follows up and consummates the deal, so to speak. You may have met and set up relationships with people who could become great bird dogs for you, but you never followed up—have you?

For those reading this right now, who have ever gone to a business after-hours gathering, I'll bet that, the next day, you couldn't even recall the name of one person you met. You have a pocketful of business cards that are meaningless. You pull them out, you look at them, and not one name is recognizable. You throw these cards in a desk drawer, telling yourself that you will email these people to tell them what a pleasure it was meeting them, and you know what? YOU WILL NEVER DO IT. BE HONEST WITH YOURSELF.

What is your first step? The key to this process is RESEARCH. Your initial step is to research. Get the Yellow Pages and the White Pages; go on the internet; get reference books; talk to people. Find the names and locations of each type of bird dog mentioned earlier and start a ledger on each one. Take a map and plot out, or draw a circle, within a 100-mile radius of the bed you sleep in at night, and start putting a pin in the map showing where each is located.

This will take work; it will take time. Don't make me spend 20 pages here telling you why you should do it, just do it. Also, when I say research, I mean research. Take every piece of information you can about a potential bird dog: name, friends, associates, size of their business, etc. It sounds hokey, but PLAN YOUR WORK AND WORK YOUR PLAN.

Now that you know whom you are looking for and where they are located, let me explain to you why you are after each one of the above and how they can make you more money—even better—how they can save you from ever having to cold call or knock on another door for the rest of your life.

REMEMBER:

AS LONG AS YOU ARE BUYING LEADS FROM SOMEONE ELSE (INTERNET LEADS ARE A VERY GOOD EXAMPLE), YOU ARE A SLAVE TO THE PERSON YOU ARE BUYING THOSE LEADS FROM. HE CONTROLS YOUR CAREER, YOU DO NOT. YOU MUST START A MARKETING PROGRAM FOR

YOURSELF WHEREBY YOU GENERATE YOUR OWN LEADS. THIS IS THE ONLY WAY YOU CAN CONTROL YOUR DESTINY. DO IT. NOW READ FURTHER.

CHAPTER Seven

Associations

Remember, in Chapter One, where I said that general advertising methods were not considered bird dog programs because they cost so much to advertise? They are an entity between the manufacturer of a product or service but they could not be included in my program because of the cost.

I went on to say that there were some areas of advertising that work, but I was one of the rare people who had discovered it in our business.

Association magazines: At one time, we advertised, using our "Affordable Life Brochure," in *Time, Newsweek, U.S. News,* etc., at $150,000 for each ad, and accidentally discovered that we could run that same brochure in magazines that targeted different segments of our country—for 1/50 the cost we paid for the same circulation with much better demographic selection. This was through association magazines. There are some 300,000 of them in the United States, and almost no one in our industry runs ads in them.

If you place my brochure in association magazines that target these people, you will succeed:

1. Small business owners.

2. Farming.

3. Retired military.

4. Anything to do with horses.

5. Anything to do with airplanes or boats.

6. Golf and tennis do not work, but scuba diving and skeet shooting work well.

7. Registered nurse magazines do not work, but licensed practical nursing magazines work well.

8. Don't run an ad in corporate lawyer magazines, but never hesitate to run one in a trial lawyer publication.

I am sure there are many more, but we found that, if you do your research and buy them right, these are winners. Never let this advertising take the place of our bird dog program, but if you are homebound due to sickness and can't get out, this is a winner. So, if you must fulfill your desire to advertise and have people call you, in my opinion, advertising in association magazines is the way to go. I have 16 ads, out of some 250 we developed and tried, that actually work well. These ads are included in my marketing materials that you receive when you join our agency.

CHAPTER Eight

Your Number-One Bird Dog

HEALTH INSURANCE AGENTS

You will find that licensed agents selling health insurance, pension cases, payroll deduction, disability income, etc., do not sell life insurance, or if they do, they do it reluctantly. They are, indeed, licensed to sell life insurance. When they take their state exam for one type of insurance, they usually automatically take the test for life insurance at the same time.

These agents can be terrific bird dogs, or if they want to sell the life insurance themselves, a great way for you to recruit agents underneath you.

You will see why I have picked them as your number-one potential bird dog. You can find them in the Yellow Pages, on the internet, or just by going to your state insurance website and clicking on agents information. Look for companies you know that sell these products and start dialing, for example, Blue Cross/Blue Shield agents or any one of dozens of insurance companies that specialize in selling products other than life insurance.

For instance, the number-one and number-two disability companies are Illinois Mutual and Assurity Life. The best person-to-person company is Combined Insurance Company and on and on. Center your efforts on contacting these types of agents. They are easy to find; they are the most receptive; they understand what you are attempting to accomplish, and will work closely with you, if you service them properly in the future.

Don't think that because another person sells insurance, they sell the same type of insurance that you offer. A client asks you about a type of insurance another person has to offer, so you send that client to them. They have a client who wants to buy what you sell, so they send their client to you.

This doesn't take a rocket scientist to figure out. I scratch your back if you scratch mine.

I have called on and set up relationships, as described, with as many as ten insurance agents and brokers in less than one day. Relationships that have lasted for years and were started with a simple phone call or visit (visits are much better). A cup of coffee is all it takes in most cases. Invite that man or woman broker to Denny's for a half hour and you can establish a friendship and business relationship that will last decades.

Many years ago, I went to see a gentleman who sold insurance part time and used cars at other times. I went to the car lot and ended up sitting in his rocking chair on the porch for an hour. Ten years later, I was the best man in his wedding. This came from one visit to his car lot. This man sent me over 200 clients during that decade of friendship. He died many years ago of a heart attack. I was a pallbearer in his funeral. It was one of the saddest days of my life.

HAVE YOU CAREFULLY READ WHAT I HAVE JUST SAID? THEN YOU WILL KNOW TO SEEK OUT HEALTH INSURANCE AGENTS AND ANY OTHER INSURANCE AGENT WHO DOES NOT SELL THE TYPE OF INSURANCE THAT YOU OFFER. START TONIGHT. GET OUT A PAD OF PAPER, GO TO THE YELLOW PAGES IN YOUR CITY AND START MAKING A

LIST OF NAMES AND TELEPHONE NUMBERS. YOU CAN GO TO THE INTERNET AND OTHER SOURCES LATER, BUT FOR TODAY, GO TO YELLOW PAGES AND LOOK UP HEALTH INSURANCE OR MAJOR MEDICAL INSURANCE AND YOU WILL BE SO SURPRISED AT HOW MANY LISTINGS YOU FIND. TOMORROW MORNING, PICK UP THE TELEPHONE AND START CALLING THEM, AND NOW, I WILL TELL YOU WHAT TO SAY.

Your approach: A telephone call is usually the best way to approach another insurance agent or broker. Set up a time to meet and when he asks you why you want to meet you say exactly this— MEMORIZE THIS, AS WRITTEN, AND SAY NO MORE.

> *"MR./MS._____, MY NAME IS _____. I AM CALLING TO ASK IF YOU SELL LIFE INSURANCE."*

If he says yes, then you tell him that you are looking for agents who sell only health insurance. You sell life insurance and you have clients who may be looking for health insurance, but you certainly can't send them to a competitor. Thank him for his time. Ninety percent of the time he will say, "WAIT, WHAT I MEANT TO SAY IS THAT I AM LICENSED TO SELL LIFE INSURANCE BUT I DON'T REALLY MESS WITH IT. I AM SOLELY IN THE HEALTH INSURANCE BUSINESS."

You then thank him and continue.

> *"WELL, MR./MS._____,THE REASON I'M CALLING IS BECAUSE I WOULD LIKE TO MEET WITH YOU FOR A FEW MINUTES BECAUSE I HAVE A VERY GOOD LIFE INSURANCE PRACTICE. I AM NOT INTERESTED IN WRITING THE TYPE OF BUSINESS YOU SELL. I WANT TO MEET WITH YOU TO SEE IF WE CAN WORK OUT SOME ARRANGEMENT WHEREBY I CAN SEND YOU MY CLIENTS WHO WANT TO BUY WHAT YOU*

SELL, MAKING SURE YOU ARE NOT MY COMPETITOR.

"ADDITIONALLY, MR./MS._____, I WANT YOU TO KNOW UP FRONT THAT I DO NOT WANT A COMMISSION FROM YOU. I JUST WANT TO MAKE SURE MY CLIENTS ARE DEALING WITH A REPUTABLE BROKER; YOU'LL SELL THEM THE BEST POLICY YOU HAVE AVAILABLE AND YOU WILL TREAT THEM AS IF THEY WERE A FAMILY MEMBER OF YOURS.

I MUST BE SURE YOU WILL NOT SEND MY CLIENT TO ANOTHER AGENT WHO MAY BE AN ASSOCIATE OR FRIEND OF YOURS THAT IS IN THE LIFE INSURANCE BUSINESS.

MR./MS._____, I UNDERSTAND THAT YOU ARE AN HONEST AND ETHICAL PERSON BUT FRANKLY, I ALWAYS LIKE TO TALK FACE-TO-FACE TO ANYONE WHO I AM GOING TO SEND MY CLIENTS TO. I HOPE YOU UNDERSTAND THAT. WOULD 3:00 TOMORROW BE CONVENIENT AT DENNY'S ON HWY 441 IN SMITHVILLE?"

By saying the above, you are putting the other agent into a position to where he has to sell you on the fact that he is an ethical man and won't do anything to hurt you. He is now selling you on why you should do business with him rather than the other way around. Quite brilliant, I must say. It works 99% of the time. By the time you hang up the phone and set a time to meet, the other agent is still trying to sell you on the fact that he is honest and ethical. At that point you might as well pull out a pen and piece of paper and pencil him in as your newest bird dog.

Read this carefully: Don't spend all your time initially calling on health insurance agents, devote one day that first week and thereafter. These are, by far and away, the easiest relationships to establish, and when you are out expanding into other areas of bird dogs, you might need a boost, a positive meeting.

If you are calling on mortgage brokers and you have two or three that are not interested in establishing a relationship with you, then it is time to call on a health insurance agent to get back on a positive track. For some reason, insurance agents usually don't start sending you new clients for a few weeks, even after you have called and met them one or more times to just get to know them. I don't know why it is this way.

So, if you spend all your time with other insurance agents, and you don't get any new clients from them initially, you will probably get discouraged and quit.

Don't be a quitter. The best way to not be a quitter is to be diversified in setting up your bird dogs. Stockbrokers will be addressed later but they are also a great source of high-end clients. Again, they don't start sending you business for weeks or even months. In the meantime, you have to sell insurance now, build for the future, but also spend some time on establishing bird dog relationships for new clients now.

There are two different and separate relationships that are possible here. One is where you send this insurance agent some business in the event that you have a client who asks for his type insurance, and in return, he sends you business under the same premise. However, the other type of relationship, and the one that I always prefer, is to make an arrangement for you to not only share clients, but for you to also pay him a percentage of the commission on any life insurance client whom he sends you.

Once he sends you that first client, and the policy you sell him gets issued and the commission is paid—when he gets his percentage of the commission (usually 25%), then you have a bird dog for life. You must continue to service him properly.

YOU SEND HIM SOME BUSINESS, HE SENDS YOU SOME BUSINESS. YOU PAY HIM A COMMISSION ON WHAT HE

SENDS YOU WHEN YOU MAKE A SALE, REGARDLESS OF WHETHER HE PAYS YOU ONE CENT OF COMMISSION ON WHAT HE SELLS.

DON'T WORRY ABOUT GETTING A COMMISSION ON THE CLIENTS YOU SEND HIM. YOU WILL MAKE MORE THAN ENOUGH ON WHAT YOU SELL, EVEN AFTER YOU PAY HIM A COMMISSION.

I PROMISE YOU.

IF YOU ARRANGE FOR HIM TO PAY YOU A COMMISSION ON CLIENTS YOU SEND HIM AND HE DOES NOT PAY YOU THE COMMISSION, YOU HAVE LOST A BIRD DOG FOR LIFE. IF HE NEEDS THE MONEY AND CAN'T OR WON'T PAY YOU WHAT HE OWES YOU, HE WILL AVOID YOU FOR THE REST OF HIS LIFE. SO JUST DON'T BOTHER TO SET UP A RELATIONSHIP LIKE THIS. SET UP A RELATIONSHIP WHERE YOU PAY HIM AND FORGET ABOUT THE OTHER WAY AROUND. DON'T BE GREEDY. THERE IS AN OLD SAYING DOWN SOUTH THAT "HOGS GET EATEN" AND IT'S TRUE.

YOU DO NOT CATCH A BIRD DOG BY RUNNING AFTER HIM; YOU CATCH YOUR BIRD DOG BY RUNNING AWAY FROM HIM. IF YOU DON'T BELIEVE ME, NEXT TIME YOU SEE A DOG ON THE SIDE OF THE ROAD, GET OUT OF YOUR CAR AND START RUNNING IN THE OPPOSITE DIRECTION OF THE DOG AND WATCH HIM RUN AFTER YOU. THIS SAME PREMISE WORKS IN LIFE AS WELL.

The next step is to go meet that agent. It's simple. You sit down after introducing yourself. You hand him a brochure—as always, the brochure is king. The brochure is the center point of the entire conversation. You tell the man what you want and how you want to set it up. As you are talking, telling him that you have clients who might want his products, you show him on the brochure the check boxes, especially the one showing health insurance. You tell him that we circulate millions of these brochures all over the United States. On occasion, someone who lives in his zip code will check that box, and when we get one of those, we will need a health insurance agent to call that client to sell him a policy. Also, we have a large book of clients, and on the occasion one of our clients calls asking us for health insurance, we need someone to send him to. This is why I asked to meet you, Mr./Ms. _____. I would like to have a mutually beneficial arrangement for us both. At that point he is still looking at the brochure and you make the offer.

Mr./Ms. _____, it's simple. I send you potential clients, and hopefully, you do the same for me on the life insurance side. If you agree, I will not only send you clients for health insurance, I will pay you $50 per sale or 25% of the commission.

THAT IS THE DEAL. THIS SHOULD LEAD TO A HANDSHAKE AND A NEW BIRD DOG. THIS IS NOT ROCKET SCIENCE.

This insurance broker that is now your bird dog has been passing up life insurance most of his career, not because he didn't want the commissions, primarily because he didn't understand life insurance. Now, he is making money and he likes it. In the past this agent had probably never asked a client of his to buy life insurance, but from the day you pay him his first commission, he will ask every single new client to buy life insurance. Once your relationship grows and prospers, he will begin working his existing database of clients for life insurance. This is where the big money is.

I have made as much as a quarter of a million dollars in commissions in the past from just one good health insurance agent bird dog; one agent sending me clients who want to buy life insurance. It didn't matter if I ever sent him one new health insurance client because I am paying him commission on sales I make to his clients. This is the key.

YOU MUST DEVELOP A RELATIONSHIP WHEREBY YOU NOT ONLY AGREE TO SEND HIM OR HER YOUR CLIENTS SEEKING HIS PRODUCT LINE, BUT YOU PAY HIM OR HER A COMMISSION ON CLIENTS OF THEIRS WHO BUY FROM

51

YOU. EVEN IF HE OR SHE DOESN'T AGREE TO PAY YOU A COMMISSION ON WHAT HE SELLS TO YOUR CLIENTS.

I DON'T MEAN TO KEEP BANGING ON THIS, BUT IT IS VITAL TO THE RELATIONSHIP.

Your new bird dog is probably licensed to sell life insurance, so pay him a commission on what you sell. This is the key to the relationship. The customary amount with our agents is 25% of our commission. This is fair. This is enough to pay him.

Two more things before we leave this section. There is a "Catch 22" involved with annuity agents and brokers. The number-one bird dog you will ever have is an annuity agent. They will send you more life insurance clients than almost any other type of agent except health insurance agents.

The problem lies in the fact that you want to sell annuities also. Annuity sales typically are big commissions, large lump sum commissions and you don't want to give that away. The best way I have found to handle this is to not even mention a relationship where you send him clients and he sends you clients.

The best way to approach this is to say,

"Mr./Ms. Agent, you send me anyone wanting to buy life insurance, and I will pay you 25% of the commission and I will do all the work. You do nothing but send the client to me."

In the past, I have been very successful setting up annuity bird dogs in this way, and when the subject comes up about annuities, what I have always said is,

"I do not solicit annuities. I will never mention annuities to your clients. I'm sure situations will arise when I have a client asking me about some annuity and I won't have a clue as to how I should handle it. If a situation like this comes up, I will surely refer that client to you."

This has always worked for me and it is the truth. I am not an annuity guy. If I get a client that I can't handle, I will need help and I will refer that client to this annuity agent.

The final thing to say on the subject of other insurance agent bird dogs is this—IF YOU DON'T SERVICE THIS NEW BIRD DOG, THEN YOU WILL LOSE HIM OR HER. THEY WILL BECOME TOTALLY INEFFECTIVE.

SERVICING MEANS THAT, AT A MINIMUM OF ONCE A MONTH, AND HOPEFULLY MORE OFTEN, YOU SIT DOWN AT A LOCAL COFFEE SHOP WITH THIS NEW BIRD DOG AND SPEND A LITTLE TIME WITH HIM OR HER. MAKE TIME.

Just talk. It can be about anything. Always split the tab or you pay this time, he pays next time. This is the best way to establish a friendship/relationship along with your business relationship. Otherwise, he or she will always look at you as a business associate and not a friend. The first time you meet for that cup of coffee, simply say,

"I'll get it this time, you get it the next."

YOU MUST MEET WITH YOUR BIRD DOGS OFTEN, OR THEY WON'T HUNT FOR YOU ANY LONGER. IT MAY BE A BREAKFAST OR A LUNCH OR JUST A CUP OF COFFEE. GET TOGETHER A MINIMUM OF ONCE A MONTH. DON'T WORRY ABOUT AN APPOINTMENT, JUST DROP INTO THE OFFICE. AS A LAST RESORT, PHONE HIM OR HER FOR A SHORT CHAT. THAT ISN'T NEARLY AS GOOD AS A VISIT, BUT IT'S SOMETHING.

IF YOU GET RELUCTANCE OR EXCUSES, MOVE ON BECAUSE THAT PERSON IS NOT A BIRD DOG WHO CAN BE RELIED UPON. THERE ARE A MILLION OTHERS, SO DON'T WORRY ABOUT IT. I FOUND THAT ABOUT 1 IN 5 NEW BIRD DOGS THAT I DEVELOPED BECAME REALLY PROFITABLE FOR ME—BUT ISN'T THAT WONDERFUL? FOR A DAY'S HUNTING, NETTING ONE GOOD FRIEND AND NEW

BUSINESS ASSOCIATE, ONE GOOD AGENT WHO WILL SEND YOU TENS OF THOUSANDS IN YEARLY INCOME. THIS PROCESS COSTS YOU ONLY A SMALL PERCENTAGE OF THE COMMISSION, WHICH DOESN'T EVEN COME FROM YOUR POCKET. IT COMES FROM THE INSURANCE COMPANY. ISN'T THIS A GREAT BUSINESS WE ARE IN?

In summary, any licensed insurance agent who does not sell life insurance is a potential bird dog for you. There are two ways you can develop a relationship, and if you service this new agent bird dog properly and frequently, then you have an income stream for life.

It's up to you as to how far you will go from here. Business doesn't start flowing in immediately once you set up a new bird dog. It takes nurturing, it takes work, but when that relationship starts to bloom—again what a great business we are in!

ONE LAST POINT THAT YOU MUST REALIZE: A BIRD DOG WILL GENERATE MORE BUSINESS THAN YOU EVER DREAMED YOU COULD WRITE, BUT THEY TAKE TIME TO NURTURE. I HAVE HAD AGENTS CALL ME AND SAY THAT THEY CALLED ON TEN AGENTS ON MONDAY AND THEY HAVEN'T GOTTEN ANY BUSINESS YET AND IT'S ALREADY WEDNESDAY. THEN THEY PROCEED TO TELL ME THAT MY PROGRAM DOESN'T WORK.

WELL, IT WILL NEVER WORK FOR THEM. NURTURE THESE RELATIONSHIPS. THEY WILL LAST YOU A LIFETIME. DON'T QUIT WHAT YOU ARE DOING NOW. KEEP SELLING LIKE YOU ARE NOW. WORK IN THE BIRD DOGGING GRADUALLY, AND WHEN YOU DO, ALLOW A LITTLE TIME FOR THE NEW BUSINESS TO KICK IN FOR YOU.

CHAPTER Nine

Don't Let People Cheat You

I don't know if anyone in the world has ever been cheated by others more than I have. These are some general tips for you on spotting someone who is more than likely to cheat you. Watch out!

1. The firm you are calling answers their phone with one word—marketing.

2. They use the Better Business Bureau (BBB) logo (The BBB is an organization that calls you saying, "If you don't join and pay us a substantial fee, when someone inquires about you, we will tell them that you don't belong to the BBB." This implies that because you are not a BBB member, you are an illegitimate business—a mere crook. Again, this implies that the consumer should not do business with you.

I once reported the BBB in Atlanta for this and was told by the Secretary of State of Georgia, Max Cleland, that he wished he could shut them down because they should be called EXTORTION USA.)

3. They always want all their money in advance.

4. They have a beautiful website with a high-rise building on it, implying they own a high-rise building or are in a high rent area.

5. Anyone who cannot give you references.

6. A man answers the phone.

7. They keep referring to "their president" like he is over at General Motors or something.

8. If they use the phrase—it's not our policy—when saying why they can't do something. (You should tell them, it's not your policy to spend money with people like them.)

9. They don't take credit cards. This can mean they have had customers call and cancel the charges many times because their product is lousy. Good luck. Always be on guard. Always be cautious, especially if it's an internet transaction. Most people selling a product or service on the internet are dishonest and you should avoid this method of doing business if at all possible.

Most importantly, if you get a bad feeling about someone selling you something, walk away. Sometimes you have that gut instinct telling you a situation is wrong. This is a fail-safe sign telling you to WALK AWAY.

Ten

Residential Mortgage Brokers

M ortgage brokers are a natural. Regardless of what people think, 94% of all the homes in the United States have owners who pay their payments monthly, payments that are on time and not delinquent. Many of these people are refinancing their homes at more attractive rates. As a result, mortgage brokers and S&L companies are flourishing.

As lengthy as the previous chapter concerning health insurance was, this chapter will not compare.

First: Go to the Yellow Pages or internet and search mortgage brokers, mortgage loans, home loans, etc. This will give you names and telephone numbers. Relying on the or internet is typically the best way to find a mortgage broker. Usually they do not have street level offices with big signs like, say, a property and casualty insurance agency.

Second: Make the call. You say,

> *"Hello, this is _____ and I would like to speak to a loan officer."*

The individuals you really want are the independent ones, which a lot of them are. Most work from a small office, or even from their homes.

The larger offices with many loan officers are more difficult for getting the person you really want to talk with. If it is a large firm, do all you can to get in to see the manager or owner. Some suggestions in doing this are:

"Mr./Ms._____, my name is_____. I am the regional representative for _____insurance company."

Always use the name of the most recognizable company that you represent.

"Mr./Ms._____, our company has a database of tens of thousands of policyholders. We frequently get requests for information on home loans, especially recently, concerning refinances. We do not work in this market. I have been instructed by my boss to find a reputable firm that we could refer our clients to, which is why I am calling. Do you have a minute?"

He will say, "Of course," and this is when you interview him. Yes, you read what I said correctly, you interview him.

"Mr./Ms._____, can you tell me something about your firm such as how long you have been in business?"

At this point, you will not get him to shut up, so you have to look for a spot to jump in to ask a few more questions.

"Mr./Ms._____, you obviously are what we are looking for. However, I would like to come by and meet you and see both you and your office. Would that be OK? Will tomorrow at 3:00 work for you?"

At that point, he will set a convenient time and you are on the way to a bird dog.

What you have done, just like with all the other bird dog telephone presentations, is put that man in a position to sell you on why you should do business with him, instead of the other way around. Mortgage brokers are usually better educated, with a great deal of common or street sense that is rare in most businessmen. He wants your business. He wants business that you can refer to him. This telephone presentation lasts a short time, yet it really generates results, whether it is a one man shop or a large shop with dozens of brokers. What you are saying is that you want to send him business, not the other way around.

Mortgage brokers are the number-two best bird dog for many reasons, which will become very apparent to you as time goes by. For me, they are even better than health insurance agents, if you service them properly. This current refinance boom in the United States will last for many years so don't you lose out on your part of this market.

You arrive at the appointed place at the appointed time. You ask politely to see the man you set the appointment with. The first thing you do after you shake his hand and introduce yourself is, *HAND HIM A BROCHURE. REMEMBER, THE BROCHURE IS KING IN ALL NEGOTIATIONS.*

A suggested presentation is this:

"Mr./Ms._____, each month my firm distributes millions of these brochures across this state and the United States as a whole (which we do collectively.) You have probably seen our brochure at one time or another. If you will look at the bottom left of the brochure, you will see some small boxes next to a line of information."

I want you to specifically point out the box that says, I would like information on a home mortgage. Then explain,

"Mr./Ms. _____, when one of our clients or prospective clients checks this box, and there are quite a few who do, they are asking us who we would recommend they contact for a home mortgage. That is why I am here. I

would like to see if you are the one we should be sending this business to you."

IT IS VITAL YOU WORD IT EXACTLY THIS WAY.

"Mr./Ms. _____, in addition to this, you may realize that our firm has millions of policyholders and we get many of them ask us the same thing. In fact, I intend to send out a newsletter very soon asking my clients if they want a home mortgage quote. To get to the point Mr./Ms. _____, if you would like to send this business to us, we would be honored to add you to our little family of strategic relationships, that we have all over the United States relationships with reputable firms working together for a common goal, and that is to make money."

"Now, Mr./Ms. _____, we are not asking for any commission even though we know that commission type arrangements are available through many mortgage brokers."

Which they are. Most mortgage brokers will pay you between 1/2 and 1% of the mortgage amount as a referral or finder's fee when you send them someone who receives a mortgage.

"What we would like, is when anyone asks one of your brokers for the name of someone who sells life insurance to cover their mortgage; you would consider mentioning our name, and let me add Mr./Ms. _____, 81% of all people taking out a new mortgage will buy life insurance to cover that mortgage in case of premature death. There is no reason why you and I shouldn't benefit from that need."

THIS IS THE KEY STATEMENT: Eighty-one percent of all people taking out a new mortgage will buy life insurance to cover that mortgage in case of premature death. This gives your presentation credibility. This is also the first time the mortgage broker realizes he will be missing the boat in servicing his clients if he does not send

60

you business, as well. Very few people ever ask to buy life insurance from a mortgage broker, and the man or woman you are talking to knows that, but this is to your advantage. He is promising to send you these people, but in his heart he thinks he really doesn't have to do anything to earn your referrals, but we all know he will.

IF YOU ARE SPEAKING TO A MANAGER OF A MORTGAGE OFFICE, YOU SAY,

"Mr./Ms. _____, if you agree, all we want to do is give out a few of these brochures to your brokers so they have something to give to your clients should they ask for life insurance, and by the way, state law allows us to designate$50 in finder's fees to the broker who refers the life insurance buyer to us. This is a great raise or bonus you can give to your brokers which you don't have to pay out of your own pocket."

MEMORIZE THIS BEFORE YOUR PRESENTATION. THIS IS KEY, JUST LIKE IT IS IN THE OTHER PRESENTATIONS. WE HAVE USED THIS FOR YEARS WITH PROPERTY AND CASUALTY INSURANCE AGENCY OWNERS/MANAGERS AND IT IS THE STATEMENT THAT CLOSES THE DEAL ALMOST EVERY TIME.

It's almost over. At this point he or she either agrees, at which point you tell him you would like a few minutes with each broker, to explain the program and to leave brochures. Make sure he or she knows you will not disturb them while taking a home loan application. If he or she doesn't agree, you shake hands and leave. Fifty percent of the time you will set up a relationship with this person and their firm, even if they has a similar relationship with another life insurance salesman. Do you know why you will get the business in the future? One reason: THE BROCHURE. IT IS KING AND NO ONE ELSE HAS IT.

The times they don't agree to set up a relationship with you, it isn't necessary to shake his or her hand and leave. You can always slap them in the face and tell them to kiss your rear end—JUST KIDDING.

We have completed the first two bird dog relationships: health insurance agents and mortgage brokers. Keep in mind that a successful life insurance agent only needs about a dozen good bird dogs to have a respectable six figure income, depending, of course, on how well you service them on an ongoing basis. Usually, health agents and mortgage brokers will be all you will ever need. As we continue, you will see more bird dog possibilities for relationships that look better than the ones we have already mentioned.

REMEMBER, WHILE YOU ARE ON GOOGLE AND IN THE YELLOW PAGES, LIST OUT EVERY HEALTH INSURANCE AGENT AND RESIDENTIAL MORTGAGE BROKER YOU CAN FIND. YOU WILL BE FLABBERGASTED AT HOW MANY THERE ARE. IN GEORGIA, RECENTLY, WE CHECKED WITH THE SECRETARY OF STATE'S OFFICE AND THERE ARE SOME 3400 LISTED MORTGAGE BROKERS IN THE STATE. CAN YOU IMAGINE? DON'T THINK ABOUT IT. GET OFF YOUR TAIL AND GO TO WORK. BUT RESEARCH IS ONLY A PART OF THE ENTIRE PICTURE. THE WORLD IS FULL OF PEOPLE WHO WANT TO STAY AT HOME AND PLAY WITH A COMPUTER. THAT COMPUTER HAS TAKEN AWAY THE BEST PART OF MANY PEOPLE'S LIVES. PEOPLE FORGET HOW TO TALK TO ANOTHER HUMAN BEING. DON'T LET THIS HAPPEN TO YOU. DO YOUR RESEARCH BUT GET OUT OF THE HOUSE AND SEE PEOPLE. THAT IS WHERE THE MONEY IS MADE. THERE ARE SO MANY PEOPLE, ESPECIALLY WOMEN, THAT FOR SOME REASON, THINK THERE ARE TENS OF THOUSANDS OF JOBS OUT THERE FOR PEOPLE WHO WANT TO SIT AT HOME EVERY DAY ON THE COMPUTER AND DO RESEARCH AND THEY WILL MAKE MONEY. I HAVE BEEN ON THIS EARTH FOR 61 YEARS SO FAR, I HAVE NEVER SEEN ONE JOB LIKE THIS OR MET ONE PERSON WHO MADE THEIR LIVING DOING RESEARCH AT HOME ON THE INTERNET. I AM NOT SAYING THIS ISN'T

POSSIBLE, I AM JUST SAYING I HAVE NEVER SEEN ANYONE DO THIS. SO, GET UP, DO YOUR RESEARCH, AND THEN GO OUTSIDE AND SEE PEOPLE.

Eleven

Building an Agency

You want to recruit agents. You want to have your own agency. That's wonderful. You should, but before you begin, you must really know what to do. So read this chapter carefully.

There are only four ways to build a solid life insurance marketing agency and they are:

1. Have a better company than others.

2. Have a better product than others.

3. Have a better commission than others.

4. Have a lead system that works, and if you have this, then the other three don't matter.

Since most major companies are pretty much the same, and when one comes out with a new product, all the others seem to have one also within six months, (1) and (2) really don't matter in today's market. You could have a better commission, but without a good product, you are out in the cold.

The last thing is to have a lead system that works and I do have that and most others don't. Remember what I said, insurance companies price the products. It is your job to sell. It is the job of your FMO to promote or find a way to put you in front of clients. The reason I have been so successful is because most companies and FMOs don't have a lead system.

The insurance companies do their job and you do yours, but if your FMO doesn't do theirs by having a lead system that works, you should change FMOs.

So, build your agency, but there are many things you need to know about finding agents, training, etc. Then you better have a mentor to help you. You need someone who will walk you through the land mines of this business or there is no reason for you to even start. Even as good as I am, training people to build an agency takes months, not weeks or days, and I am one of the few who knows how to do it.

Twelve

Property and Casualty Insurance Agencies

Mainstream property and casualty insurance agencies are the number-three bird dogs. They are a twelve-month source of leads. People have already bought some type of insurance from them so you don't have a credibility problem with the prospect when you call for an appointment. Just one agency can send you enough life business to generate you as much as $25,000 or more in income each year if you set them up right from the beginning, and service them correctly on an ongoing basis.

It is not difficult to designate which agencies you want to target. Don't waste your time with State Farm agents. Whether they sell life insurance or not, they are not allowed to have anything to do with other companies and if they do, they lose their jobs. State Farm agents are the highest paid insurance agents, overall, in the country and they will not jeopardize this standard of living for anyone. Just leave them alone.

There are others like State Farm that will not do business with you, including Farm Bureau, Cotton States, and National Auto.

DON'T BOTHER TO CALL ON AUTOMOBILE-ONLY INSURANCE AGENCIES. SOME ARE KNOWN AS

SUBSTANDARD AUTO AGENCIES. THEY ONLY HANDLE LOW-INCOME CLIENTS WHO, ON THE WHOLE, HAVE NO CHECKING ACCOUNTS, NO CREDIT CARDS OR ANY MEANS OF PAYING FOR LIFE INSURANCE, EVEN IF YOU SELL THEM A POLICY. THEY ARE EASY TO SET UP. JUST WALK INTO ONE, GIVE OUR FAMOUS 2-MINUTE PRESENTATION, AND 9 TIMES OUT OF 10, THEY WILL SIGN UP WITH YOU— BUT THEN YOU SPEND TIME AND MONEY AND YOU NEVER GET ONE DECENT LEAD OUT OF THEM. I PERSONALLY SET UP AN AGENCY IN ATLANTA THAT HAD 51 OFFICES. THE FIRST WEEK WE GOT 60 LEADS AND NOT ONE TURNED INTO A SALE. DO NOT WASTE YOUR TIME.

Along the same line, some agents assume that other agencies similar to State Farm are just as difficult to target, but you would be surprised. Allstate agencies are a large source of leads for us. Most of their agents are unhappy.

They are having a tough time making a living. They are pressured to sell life insurance but the commission is so low, they can't make enough money to justify the work they do. They also know that their company will not take most impairment, so even if they do write a policy, there is a good chance that, unless the prospect is in perfect health, it will not go through.

YOU PRESENT OUR OPPORTUNITY THIS WAY…

"Mr./Ms. (agency owner), we know that there are a great many risks your company does not want to accept concerning life insurance. This is what we do. We work with many captive P&C agencies across the United States on the cases they can't place, cases such as insulin dependent diabetics, heart bypass cases, severe high blood pressure and other illnesses. We have a place and a way to write most of them."

"We know that your company allows most of their agencies to place life insurance business outside of their company, if it is a type person they do not want to insure.

68

We would like the business, and in return, we will do our best to send you business."

"This is our brochure. If you will take a few seconds to look it over, you will see that on the left flap are a number of boxes that can be checked if one of our life insurance prospects is interested in other things, such as car, homeowners, business insurance. We do not sell these types of insurance. Would you like us to send them to you?"

From this point on, you will follow the standard presentation in the chapter on bird dog presentations.

I have covered much of the telephone pitch and the face-to-face presentation in the sections on health insurance and mortgage brokers.

Property and casualty agencies are just about like those. There is no sense belaboring the point. Mainstream independent property and casualty insurance agencies are what most of us are familiar with. They sell homeowners, auto, boat and business insurance. They are the mainstay of the business. Most legitimate ones belong to the "Big I" or the national association of independent insurance agencies, a very reputable association.

Let's give this a once around. Memorize every word of the script that follows. Don't wing it. Do not guess at it. If you say exactly what I'm saying below, you will be successful. First, you call; talk to the receptionist or one of the people working out front whose responsibility it is to answer the phone and you say this:

"Hello, my name is _____. My wife and I are new to the area and I am calling to see what companies you sell auto and homeowners with. Then you say, by the way, my wife has been after me to buy some life insurance. Do you sell life insurance?"

When she says no, you ask,

"Do you recommend someone I can call to buy life insurance?"

When she says no again, YOU HAVE A WINNER. YOU HAVE AN AGENCY TO CALL ON.

All you need to do now is find out the owner's name. Then, a couple of days later you call and say,

"Can I speak to Mr./Ms._____?"

They will ask why and you say this to the receptionist, and you will repeat this to the owner once you are put on the phone.

"Mr./Ms._____, my name is _____and I am a regional general agent with Mutual of Omaha. The reason I am calling is that my boss asked me to call and say that we have an extremely large life insurance, annuity, and pension practice."

IT'S IMPORTANT YOU SAY IT JUST LIKE THIS BECAUSE THE ANNUITY AND PENSION PHRASE GIVES YOU CREDIBILITY THAT LIFE INSURANCE DOES NOT.

"We have tens of thousands of clients, and on occasion, one will ask us if we sell auto or homeowners insurance. More times than not, it's one of our small business owner clients asking us for a referral to someone who writes business insurance. We are looking for an agency to send our clients to, but we must make sure they are reputable and solid. Mr./Ms._____, someone recommended you to my boss, I don't know who, and the reason I am calling is to ask you how long you have been in business, and what companies you represent."

HE OR SHE WILL SPEND THE NEXT FIFTEEN MINUTES, IF YOU LET THEM, SELLING YOU ON THE FACT THEY ARE HONEST AND LEGITIMATE.

You then say,

"Mr./Ms._____, I would like to come by and visit with you for a few minutes in person, would tomorrow at 3:00 be OK?"

You will get that appointment. This is the second step, research first, then set an appointment and do not deviate. Don't play from the hip, you type out what I just wrote and place it on a piece of paper, read it off when you talk to the agent.

STEP THREE: YOU WALK INTO THE FRONT DOOR OF THE AGENCY. YOU HAND EVERYONE YOU SEE A BROCHURE, REMEMBER, FOR THE TENTH TIME, THE BROCHURE IS KING. YOU GO UP TO THE RECEPTIONIST, INTRODUCE YOURSELF, ASK IF THEM IF THEY ARE THE OWNER. THIS IS VERY IMPORTANT BECAUSE IT MAKES THEM FEEL IMPORTANT.

YOU ASK FOR THE OWNER, TELLING THE RECEPTIONIST YOU HAVE AN APPOINTMENT. YOU ARE USHERED INTO THE OWNER'S OFFICE. YOU HAND HIM OR HER A BROCHURE AND THEY WILL PROMPTLY START READING THE RATES FOR THEIR SELF AND FAMILY MEMBERS WHILE YOU TALK. YOU MAKE SURE YOU HAVE A POSTER WITH YOU, BUT DON'T SHOW IT TO THE OWNER YET. YOU BEGIN YOUR SIXTY-SECOND PRESENTATION AND THIS IS IT:

"Mr./Ms._____, as I said on the phone, I am_____and I am a regional representative with Mutual of Omaha. I'm sure I don't have to tell you who we are. My boss asked me to come by today to see you. If you will notice on the brochure you have in your hand, on the bottom left side, there are several short questions and one of them is asking our clients if they are interested in a quote for homeowner, auto, or business insurance. It will surprise you how many of our business clients and middle to upper income families check that box."

"To get to the point Mr./Ms._____, we have tens of thousands of clients in this state and many of them frequently call us for property and casualty insurance. We do not sell it, but we feel we are doing them a disservice if we don't at least help them find a reputable agency. In addition, we put out millions of these brochures and a great many people who want a quote on their homeowners, auto, etc., many right here in this area, check that box. You were recommended to my boss, he sent me to see what I think of your agency. I sure can tell you that you look busy and prosperous and this would not be if you were not a competitive and solid agency.

Can you tell me a little about yourself?"

AT THIS POINT, GET COMFORTABLE, BECAUSE LIKE MOST PEOPLE, THEIR FAVORITE SUBJECT IS THEMSELVES. TRY TO CUT HIM OFF AFTER 15 to 20 MINUTES AND SAY,

"Well, it sure looks like you are exactly what we are looking for. I must know if we are sending our clients to a competitor, Mr./Ms. _____. Do you sell life insurance or do you have someone you send your clients to that sells life insurance?"

You already know the answer, he says no and then you add:

"Mr./Ms._____, if you are interested in providing a great life insurance carrier to your agency, we would like to apply for the job. It's simple. Here is one of our posters that we put on the wall in the waiting area of most agencies we work with. It's just a blown up version of our brochure you have in your hand."

IT IS VERY IMPORTANT YOU TAKE A POSTER WITH YOU. IT IS IMPRESSIVE AND MOST P&C AGENCY OWNERS LOVE THINGS LIKE THIS.

"In addition, we will give to each of your employees out front a few of these brochures, like the one I just gave you, and when someone comes in asking for life insurance, we sure would appreciate it if they would give one to your customer. That's it sir. This is sort of a, you scratch my back and we will scratch yours."

One-third of the time the agency owner will buy a life insurance policy from you.

"Mr./Ms._____, we need some of your business cards, any brochures you may have and we will give a few of ours to your employees. If that's OK, then I will be on my way and I would like to know if it's OK for me to drop by on occasion to say hello."

HE WILL SAY YES TO EVERYTHING AND YOU ARE ON YOUR WAY.

Now, the next important step. Remember, hardly anyone walks in asking for life insurance and that is one of the reasons the owner will allow you to put out brochures. He thinks this is an easy way to get rid of you and get you out of his office. Boy, oh boy, is he wrong!

You take each employee in the office, including the janitor, and you spend a few minutes with each one of them. Without this step, you might as well not go into the joint in the first place. Now you say,

"Hello, I just met with your owner and I am your new life insurance agent. Here are some of our life insurance brochures."

By now, he or she has already looked at the brochure, studied the chart, and is ready to ask questions. When they are finished, you say,

"We would appreciate it if you would hand out the brochure to clients who come in."

You mention, on the average, one in sixteen will buy a life insurance policy from us, and if they do, you will be paid a $25 referral fee, simply by asking,

"WOULD YOU LIKE TO ADD SOME LOW-COST TERM LIFE INSURANCE THROUGH MUTUAL OF OMAHA TO YOUR COVERAGE?"

That's it. No, we don't bill along with their other insurance, but we do take a check for a draft on their account or we will bill on a Q, S/A, or an A basis. Remember,

"WOULD YOU LIKE TO ADD SOME LOW-COST TERM LIFE INSURANCE THROUGH MUTUAL OF OMAHA TO YOUR COVERAGE?"

***NOT: "DO YOU WANT TO BUY SOME LIFE INSURANCE," BUT "WOULD YOU LIKE TO ADD SOME LOW-COST TERM LIFE INSURANCE THROUGH MUTUAL OF OMAHA TO YOUR COVERAGE," AND HAND THEM A BROCHURE.

Explain that you pay every Friday. If we get a card from you, a fax, or a call, we will drop by and pick it up. The card should be filled out in receptionist's handwriting. When we sell that person, then they will get the referral fee. That's it.

Remember, HAND THEM A BROCHURE, THEN ASK THEM: WOULD YOU WANT TO ADD SOME LOW-COST LIFE INSURANCE TO YOUR COVERAGE WITH MUTUAL OF OMAHA? YOU FILL OUT THIS APPLICATION REQUEST FORM. CALL FOR US TO PICK IT UP OR FAX THE CARD TO US. THAT'S IT AND WHEN ISSUED, WE BRING YOU A CHECK FOR $25.

Remember, $25 is going to the agency and $25 to the individual.

READ VERY, VERY, VERY CAREFULLY. IF YOU DON'T DO THIS DURING THE NEXT FEW DAYS, YOU MIGHT AS WELL NEVER GO INTO THIS PLACE TO BEGIN WITH.

YOU WILL NOT GET MANY, IF ANY, LEADS THE FIRST WEEK AFTER YOU SET THEM UP. THOSE EMPLOYEES OUT FRONT ARE NOT ASKING ANYONE TO BUY LIFE

INSURANCE, ESPECIALLY SINCE, AFTER YOU HAVE READ ALL THIS SO FAR, YOU ARE PROBABLY GOING TO FINISH WITH THE OWNER, THEN WALK TO THE OUTER OFFICE AND SAY,

"HELLO, I AM _____, AND THE OWNER TOLD ME IT WAS OK TO PUT A FEW OF THESE BROCHURES AROUND HERE ON THE COUNTER. THANK YOU AND SEE YOU LATER."

AS FUNNY AS THIS SOUNDS, THIS IS EXACTLY WHAT ABOUT FOUR OUT OF FIVE READING THIS RIGHT NOW WILL DO, AND YOU WILL NOT GET THE FIRST LEAD FROM THIS AGENCY. SO FOR THE ONE IN FIVE WHO WILL SIT DOWN WITH EACH EMPLOYEE AND GO OVER EVERYTHING AND WORK WITH THEM A WHILE BEFORE LEAVING, YOU STILL WON'T GET ANYTHING MUCH THAT FIRST WEEK UNTIL YOU DO THIS:

YOU GO BACK IN THREE OR FOUR DAYS. TAKE A CUP OF COFFEE OR A DOUGHNUT. SHOW THAT YOU CARE ENOUGH ABOUT THEM TO BRING THEM SOMETHING BESIDES YOUR SMILING FACE.

THEN YOU ASK IF YOU CAN SIT AROUND FOR A LITTLE WHILE AND HAND A FEW LIFE INSURANCE BROCHURES OUT TO THEIR CUSTOMERS WHO COME IN. AND I HAVE NEVER IN 20 YEARS HAD ANYONE TO TELL ME NO. EVERY PERSON WHO WALKS IN THE DOOR YOU GET UP, INTRODUCE YOURSELF AND SAY,

"I am the agency's life insurance agent. Here is a brochure on our latest low-cost term life insurance with Mutual of Omaha. Would you like us to add some low-cost life insurance to your coverage?"

Now, we know they can't bill it along with their car insurance but that doesn't matter. It's all in how you phrase it. Phrase it this way, just like you taught the office employees to say it, and you will have a minimum of 1 in 17 people who will say, "Why yes, I do need some life insurance." In many cases, if you especially ask all the women who come into the place if they would like to buy some life insurance on themselves or THEIR HUSBANDS, then you will walk away with two sales.

I GET SO FRUSTRATED TRYING TO BEAT THIS INFORMATION INTO AGENTS' HEADS. EIGHTY PERCENT OF THE TIME THEY JUST SIT AND STARE AT ME, LISTEN, THEN SAY, "Oh yes, Mr. Murray, I got this."

So you wait around, make a call with them, sit in the outer office when they come out of the owner's office and you just sit and watch them flop some brochures on the counter and walk out. Nothing else is required, not a word to the employees out front. You think that is unusual. It truly is not.

EIGHTY PERCENT OF THE AGENTS I TRAIN WILL DO THIS AND THEN IN A WEEK THEY CALL ME SAYING WHAT WE DO DOES NOT WORK AND I GET SO MAD...SO FRUSTRATED.

OK, property and casualty agencies are the number-three best bird dogs as long as they are full service and you set them up and service them properly. Make your list from Google or research them.

Make the setup call. Make the appointment call. Go see the owner or manager and do not be scared off if they have more than one office. Those are the easiest.

If you don't do anything else but walk in off the street, ask to see the owner and say,

"Sir/Ma'am, we would like for you to contract with us."

When he tells you that he is pressured from his homeowner insurance companies to sell life insurance, you listen, and when he shuts up, you say,

"Well, if someone comes in wanting to buy, and you are so busy you don't want to mess with it, call us."

76

We do all the work and still pay him a commission. FOLLOW THIS AND YOU WILL SET UP 1 IN 5 YOU CALL ON. Property and Casualty Insurance Agencies are a wonderful source of new-client sales for years to come.

CHAPTER *Thirteen*

"It really doesn't matter what you say, it's how you say it."

— Jerry Clower, Comedian, January 1994

My second-best friend growing up was Sonny Allgood. His dad was the State of Georgia sales rep for Bush Hog Corporation. In case you don't know what that is, a Bush Hog is a piece of heavy farm equipment used primarily for cutting weeds or plowing fields.

Sonny and his dad invited me to accompany them on a road trip to Alabama one year during Christmas vacation. It was wonderful. It was one of the rare vacations for me away from having to work at my father's store.

Now, at one of the stops, at a dealer that sold Bush Hogs, I stood there watching and listening to Mr. Allgood make his sales pitch to the owner. He said, "Now, Mr. Sheriff, a man of your rank and smell should have at least five of these cutter units on your yard out here. You can't sell 'em if you ain't got 'em."

The man looked at him and said, "OK. Unload them."

When we got back into the Chevrolet El Camino he drove, we pulled off and I couldn't help it. I asked Mr. Allgood what he meant by "rank and smell." What did that mean? He smiled and said, "Son, I have no idea, but at the time, it sure sounded good."

My Lord, I thought, some men would have knocked his head off for saying that, but Mr. Allgood could not only say it, he got away with it. This taught me a good lesson in life. It's not necessarily what you say but how you say it.

This carries a message to you to say the right thing if you can but if you can't or don't, then just stare that other person in the eye and don't bat an eyelash.

NOW, ON TO THE NEXT CHAPTER.

Fourteen

Tax Preparation Services, Bookkeepers and CPAs

Bookkeepers, CPAs, and tax preparation services are not at the top of the list of potential bird dogs. Once you work their current block of business, bookkeepers and CPAs really have no one to send you and once the four months of tax season is over, tax prep offices have nothing to send you for 8 months. They are not month-after-month, year-long bird dogs that can send you clients on a regular basis like a property and casualty insurance agency or a mortgage broker. Let's take these one by one.

TAX PREPARATION OFFICES

H & R Block is the best known, but this isn't who we want as our bird dog in a particular area. We want the other independents like Liberty Tax Preparation Services and others. They are usually owned by one person and that person usually has three or four locations. Tax prep offices love what we have to offer. The actual person doing the tax return is paid a standard $29 for preparation of a return so when we offer them $50 for every sale we make on someone they send us, they jump at the chance. The owner's presentation is similar to all the others, but remember that key phrase you must memorize.

THE MONEY WE PAY TO THE TAX PREPARATION PEOPLE IN YOUR OFFICE IS A BONUS THEY RECEIVE THAT DOESN'T COME OUT OF YOUR POCKET.

This phrase is the clincher in most cases. They don't pay these people much. They have a high turnover. If there is something to cut down on attrition, then they are for it and our fee to them is that clincher.

BOOKKEEPERS AND CPAS

Most of them have a block of a few dozen small business owners as clients. Don't think the $50 finder's fee isn't important. They love to make money. Most are very jealous of some of their clients. Over the years, I wish I had a dollar for every time I heard a CPA or bookkeeper say to me, "That client of mine is so stupid and he makes so much money. I am in the wrong business." Most all are really jealous of their clients' successes.

They are really envious of their clients and every penny they can make is one penny that no longer separates them from people they believe are not as smart as they are. The main problem is that once you work their clients, there really isn't anything else to do, except maybe, on rare occasion in years to come, they will refer a new client to you. However, in the meantime, they can be quite lucrative. The best story I can tell you is: Mike Tracy in Corpus Christi, Texas, was driving down a street one late afternoon in 2008 and spotted a sign for a bookkeeping service. He stopped, went in, and made a brief presentation to a lady who owned the service. He said she was not in the least enthusiastic about what he offered, but agreed to let him leave some brochures on the table.

A week later, Mike was going by that location and wasn't intending to stop, but he had an hour to kill and thought, what the heck. So he went in and was greeted with a smile and warm welcome by the lady. She had him sit down next to her at the desk while she went over sheet after sheet listing all her clients and what they wanted. She had called every single client and asked them to buy life insurance. She told them what it cost from the brochure Mike had left with her and they told her how much they wanted on themselves, their family, and their employees.

Bookkeepers, and CPAs especially, carry a great deal of weight and have a lot of influence with their clients and this was no exception.

The lady had 101 clients of which 90 had told her that they would buy life insurance on themselves and others. The total policy count was 277 policies. Mike got the list, their names, how much coverage they wanted, their contact information, notes as to the best time to call them and off he went. Mike wrote over $100,000 in first-year commission from this one account, and to the best of my knowledge, is still writing business from this bird dog. Mike was smart to get referrals from every client of hers that he wrote and he will have enough people to go see for years to come. This is the best definition of a true BIRD DOG I have ever seen.

IS THIS UNUSUAL? OF COURSE, BUT IT DOES HAPPEN MORE THAN YOU WILL EVER KNOW. A broker of mine in McLean, Virginia, once met a man at a cocktail party in Washington, D.C., at the Israeli Embassy. He handed the man a brochure because he didn't have a business card with him. Ten days later, he began enrolling 106 people, all members of the National Symphony Orchestra, for a 20-year term, $100,000 life insurance policy. It turns out the man he met was the conductor and he was shopping for this coverage for his people, met my man, was so impressed that he could look at our brochure and tell what was going on, that he bought. The commission was almost $96,000, and every time they hired a new fiddle player, my broker wrote a policy. That was 19 years ago and he still has the account. IS THIS UNUSUAL? OF COURSE, BUT IT DOES HAPPEN MORE THAN YOU WILL EVER KNOW.

A broker of mine in Atlanta, Georgia, left some brochures at a full-service car wash located near the intersection of Druid Hills Road and Interstate 85 and told the cashier he would pay her $50 for every sale she sent him. Six months later, with no sales yet, but my broker going by religiously once or twice a month to get his car washed, a man came through in a Bentley one day. He picked up a brochure and asked the girl how to contact the agent. She called my broker right then and put him on phone. They set up an appointment the next week. I am ashamed to say this, but my broker almost didn't go. But he did and walked away with sales that, over the next three months, amounted to almost $84,000 in first-year commission. It turns out, the man owned the largest record company in the southeastern United States. IS THIS UNUSUAL? OF COURSE, BUT IT DOES HAPPEN MORE THAN YOU WILL EVER KNOW. I HAVE HUNDREDS OF STORIES JUST LIKE THIS.

How do you proceed? Always try to set up an appointment, if possible.

Most CPAs will not see you without one. When you call, say,

"Mr./Ms._____, my name is _____, and I am the regional representative for_____ in this part of the state of _____."

You say it this way because they want to do business with important people and the more important your title is, the more credibility they give you.

"I am calling because we need your help. Mr./Ms._____, we do business with thousands of all business owners across the state."

THEY LOVE SMALL BUSINESS OWNERS. THAT IS WHERE THE MONEY IS, NOT IN DOING TAX RETURNS.

"Many of them ask us on occasion who we would recommend as a reputable accountant and frankly, I don't know what to tell the ones in this area. I don't personally

know any accountants. Your name was given to me as a highly reputable and knowledgeable person in your business and I am calling to see if we could share a few minutes together sometime, so I might see if you could be the one I recommend to my clients."

That's it. He will most always say yes. You go see that man or woman, take a brochure and hand it to him or her when you walk inside. You give the same presentation changing only a word or two here and there and better than 75% of the time you will establish a relationship with the bookkeeper and 1/3 of the time you will do the same with the CPA. In many cases, the bookkeeper is much smarter than the CPA but it's an ego thing. Most CPAs have been approached so many times by life insurance agents for a similar arrangement, they are cold to anything you might say. However, most "big time" insurance agents like New York Life or Northwestern Mutual also have big egos and they think they are too good to be seen with a lowly bookkeeper.

You will find there are several national franchises for bookkeepers like Padgett Business Services or General Business Services. It's easy to find out who they are by just going online and putting in your state. Up come all their representatives, but most are independent.

REMEMBER, THE BROCHURE IS KING. Once they are set up, SERVICE IS WHAT KEEPS THEM. Take them to lunch. They'll go. Everyone loves a free lunch. It is often difficult to get them to step out of the office for a cup of coffee, but early breakfast or lunch will work. Our history with this type of bird dog is that CPAs are good bird dogs, but bookkeepers are GREAT!

Do not hesitate to specialize and concentrate on bookkeepers. In December, before tax season, remember to set up your tax prep offices. Tax preparation offices can be a tremendous source of referrals to you.

Do your research, make a presentation and give them service. You will have a steady flow of new clients coming from CPAs, bookkeepers, and tax preparation offices for years to come.

I HAVE KNOWN SALES TO BE MADE BECAUSE OF AN ACCOUNTANT'S OR BOOKKEEPER'S REFERRAL THAT EASILY AMOUNTED TO $10,000 OR MORE IN FIRST-YEAR COMMISSIONS.

THESE ARE A VALUABLE SOURCE OF NEW SALES. DO NOT BE SCARED OFF BECAUSE YOU SOMEHOW THINK THAT THESE PEOPLE ARE UNTOUCHABLE, OR TOO POWERFUL. THEY PUT ON THEIR PANTS JUST LIKE YOU AND ME.

Fifteen

Stay Motivated

I have a friend, a broker, who has worked with me for many years. He is a nephew of a famous professional football player. His uncle was asked to go on a television program with a famous motivator, a man who was known for selling motivational programs to the general public.

The advertisement for this man's motivational course was made into an infomercial and was filmed around a swimming pool in Hawaii. This was to ensure an upscale crowd for an audience.

My friend's uncle was brought on shortly after the beginning of the commercial. He testified that his life had been changed by the man selling the motivational courses. He went on to say he wouldn't have thrown that winning touchdown pass in the Super Bowl had it not been for his tapes and books. I understand this man who sells his programs to the public is very successful because of many reasons, including his message.

My friend told me that every time the family watches this infomercial, they just roll on the floor, laughing. "Why?" I asked.

He told me that his uncle had not even heard of this man until a week before the filming of the commercial and had never met him in person until thirty minutes before the show. This is what, in my opinion, most of these self-promoters have for you and others, nothing but air.

The point I am trying to make is that you can get motivated for a day or two by going to a seminar or by reading a book or listening to a CD by one of these motivators, but it runs out. You must learn to motivate yourself.

Do not rely on these people who do not know specifics about our business.

Do you want to get motivated? Then get up and go to work. Put in 8 hours going out and meeting strangers for just one day. Just 8 hours. Take a handful of brochures and walk up to one hundred strangers, hand them one, and ask them to buy life insurance, and at five o'clock, you will have made one, two, three or more sales and put $500, $1,000, $2,000 or more in your pocket. I have had brokers who worked with me over the years who do this every day of their lives. One, a personal friend and broker who has worked with me for some 20 years, goes to five or six Denny's restaurants every day during the week. He sits down, orders coffee, then gets up and hands every person in the restaurant a brochure and asks them to buy life insurance from him. In 2008, he made $400,000 in first-year commissions and 90% of it came from his restaurant sales. So, don't tell me ever that you can't make a living. Don't tell me the economy is bad. It is bad, but 90% of the people still have jobs and make the same income, or more, as they always have, so just get up, do the bird dog program and make more money than you ever dreamed of.

Sixteen

Always Be Prepared

D o you remember the miniseries some years back called "Band of Brothers?" I'm sure most of you reading this recall. Well, if you remember, their war cry was "CURRAHEE!" and that came from my home town, Currahee Mountain, located just five miles from Toccoa, where I grew up. During WWII, this was the training camp for paratroopers going into the war in Europe. This entire movie's first three segments were about this camp. Unfortunately, they didn't film it in Toccoa.

It was filmed in England because Tom Hanks, the producer, said that our area didn't look much like a training camp to him. You can't win them all.

In those days, most of the soldiers traveled by train, and that train, the *Southern Crescent* went all the way from New Orleans to Boston and right through the middle of Toccoa, Georgia. This may have been one reason they chose Toccoa as the site of their camp, but it really doesn't matter.

At our train depot was a dirty little café called Powers Café, owned and run by Henry Powers. He was a "salty" old dude who never married, but that is not what set him apart from others. When he was a young boy, Henry shot off his chin in a hunting accident and leaving him mightily deformed.

You could hardly look at the man. You didn't laugh, either, or that man would pull out a gun and threaten you. I don't know if he actually killed anyone for laughing, and I didn't want to find out, either.

His café was dark and dreary, but most of the soldiers getting off the train in Toccoa would usually end up sitting, drinking a cup of coffee while they waited for their transportation to the camp. However, this has nothing to do with the story I am writing here.

One morning, Henry left his house for work. He always left home at 4:00 a.m. and opened his café at 4:30 a.m. Henry didn't believe in banks. He carried every penny in the world he had in a suitcase that he carried with him to work every day, and he never took his eye off of it. For those of you younger folks reading this book, believe what I'm telling you, because that Depression of the 1930's scared many folks away from banks.

Henry went out the front door of his house, carrying that suitcase full of money, and out from the bushes jumped a man with a blackjack, intent on hitting Henry over the head and stealing his suitcase and his money.

Before the man could come down, holding the blackjack, Henry whirled around in the dark, and shot the man between the eyes, twice, with his .45 caliber pistol.

Later on in the morning, the neighbors, on their way to work, saw a man lying out in Henry's front yard and called the police, who investigated and then headed for the cafe. "What happened, Henry?" they asked. Well, old Henry proceeded to tell them what had happened, when the obvious question came up.

"Henry, in pitch dark, loaded down with a heavy suitcase, looking for your car keys, you were able to shoot this man squarely between the eyes and kill him. Now, Henry, how did you know he was there?"

"WELL," HENRY SAID, "I'VE BEEN WAITING ON THE S.O.B. FOR THIRTY YEARS!"

That is being prepared. That is what you must do. Always be prepared for any situation that may come up in a sales situation. Know what to say, but most of all...in this book, I tell you in some places to memorize what I tell you to say and be prepared.

Memorize it or you won't be successful.

Seventeen

Savings and Loan
and Bank Loan Officers

S AVINGS AND LOAN AND BANK LOAN OFFICERS ARE A TERRIFIC SOURCE OF LEADS AND HERE IS HOW YOU APPROACH AND SET THEM UP.

Do not go to the president. Do not make a presentation to the manager. If you do, you are wasting your time. Walk in to a bank or savings and loan. You can tell who the loan officers are because they sit in one of those glass cubicles. They hate this, because most of them never do any work and they can't hide. Everyone in the bank, everyone who comes into the bank, sees that they don't do anything, so when you come in and want to see them, they are thrilled because it makes them look like they are doing something.

If there is a secretary, ask to speak to the loan officer. They won't ask you why. They assume you are looking for a loan. If they don't have a secretary acting as their gatekeeper, then you just walk right in and you say,

"Hello, my name is _____. I am an area supervisor for Mutual of Omaha."

(Remember, we do represent Mutual of Omaha, we do sell business with them, and they have the most recognizable name. Their name gives us credibility.)

"We work with quite a few loan executives (Don't say loan officer. It bruises their ego.) in this area and throughout the state. Here is one of our flyers illustrating some of our very low-cost term life insurance products."

Hand him a brochure, and while you finish your presentation, he will look at how much he can buy at his age. They always do this when you hand them a brochure.

FOR THE TENTH TIME, THE BROCHURE IS KING. DO EVERYTHING YOU CAN TO GET IT INTO THEIR HANDS AS SOON AS YOU ENTER.

"Sir, when you make a loan to someone and you feel the bank would be at risk if that person were to die before the loan is paid off, we would appreciate a call. Please take a few of our brochures (hand him half dozen or so), *and keep them handy, if you would be so kind."*

"In return, for you sending us business, we will do our best to send you our clients who are looking for business loans."

Then you say,

"A high percentage of our clients are small business owners."

That's it! Just say this and point out on the application return card where there is a box for someone to check if they are looking for a bank loan or banking relationship.

"Mr./Ms. Bank Executive, state law allows Mutual of Omaha to pay a $50 referral fee to you, or if you want, we can pay it to the bank."

Most of the time, he says he does not want his money to go to the bank.

You just found a new bird dog.

"Mr./Ms. Bank Executive, our firm distributes millions of these brochures just like the one I just handed to you, primarily in MasterCard and Visa bills. We recently put out 1.1 million in a Wells Fargo Visa statement.

(We did that recently).

"When we get a card back where someone has checked this box (point out the box where it says business loans), *then you sure will get your fair share of them."*

***THIS IS THE KEY—

"But, Mr./Ms. Bank Executive, you need to tell me what type of loans you are looking for!"

ABOUT WHAT HE OR SHE DOES, ABOUT HIS OR HER BANK, ABOUT THE TYPE OF LOANS THEY WANT. THIS GIVES HIM OR HER A CHANCE TO TALK AND THESE GUYS LOVE HEARING THE SOUND OF THEIR OWN VOICE MORE THAN ANYTHING IN THE WORLD, AND TO THE OUTSIDE WORLD STANDING IN THEIR LOBBY. IT MAKES THEM LOOK LIKE THEY ARE DOING SOMETHING. THEY LOVE SAYING TO OTHER BANK EMPLOYEES WHEN THEY CALL UPON HIM OR HER FOR SOMETHING, "I'M WITH A CUSTOMER, PLEASE CALL LATER." THIS ONE STATEMENT IS THE KEY. MEMORIZE IT:

BUT YOU NEED TO TELL ME WHAT TYPE OF LOANS YOU ARE LOOKING FOR.

After the bank executive finishes talking, it is assumed that he or she will send you life insurance clients. The banker will usually say, "Well, Mr./Ms. Life Insurance Agent, would you please give me a few more brochures? I will keep them in my desk and give them to my customers."

THEY WILL SAY THIS, AS WELL. ABOUT ONE TIME IN THREE, THEY WILL ASK YOU ABOUT LIFE INSURANCE FOR THEMSELVES AND THEIR FAMILY, AND THEY WILL BUY LIFE INSURANCE ON THEMSELVES AND THEIR FAMILY ALMOST EVERY TIME. ONE IN TWO BANK LOAN OFFICERS, IF APPROACHED IDENTICALLY TO WHAT I HAVE SAID ABOVE, WILL BECOME A BIRD DOG FOR YOU AND ONE IN THREE TIMES, HE OR SHE WILL BUY A LIFE INSURANCE POLICY FOR THEIRSELF AND THEIR FAMILY.

IN SUMMARY, THIS IS EXACTLY WHAT YOU SHOULD MEMORIZE, AND I MEAN IT. IF YOU DON'T MEMORIZE IT, YOU WILL NOT BE SUCCESSFUL.

> *"Hello, Mr./Ms. Bank Executive, My name is _____. I am the regional supervisor for Mutual of Omaha. We work with a great many financial executives in the area and across the state. Here is one of our low-cost term life insurance brochures."*

> *"Mr./Ms. Bank Executive, when you make a loan to someone and you feel the bank would be at risk if that person dies before the loan is paid off, we would appreciate a call. In return, we will send you as many small business owners as we can who are looking for a new banking relationship or a loan, and under state law, we will pay you a referral fee of $50. You can pass this on to the bank if you wish."*

> *"Mr./Ms. Bank Executive, do you think you could take a minute or two and tell me about your bank and the type loans you are looking for?"*

THE REST JUST HAPPENS EXACTLY AS I SAID. YOU LEAVE SOME BROCHURES, FILL OUT THE APPLICATIONS FOR INSURANCE ON HIM AND HIS FAMILY THEN YOU WALK THROUGH THE BANK, TO THE OTHER LOAN OFFICERS, ALL THE WHILE HANDING OUT BROCHURES TO

THE OTHER BANK EMPLOYEES, AND DON'T MISS A ONE OF THEM.

You have an added advantage with savings and loan officers. They not only make business loans, they also make mortgage loans. So when showing them the check boxes on the brochure, point out both the business loans, SBA loans and the mortgage loan check boxes. It can make the difference between establishing a bird dog or not.

For some reason, it is pretty easy to sell a bank loan officer a policy, but it is rare to have a savings and loan officer buy a policy from you. I don't know why. Maybe it's because that, as lazy as bank loan officers can be, savings and loan officers have less to do, so they don't have as much time to think about dying as others do. It really doesn't matter.

SERVICE IS KING, BUT YOU DON'T NEED TO TAKE ANYONE TO LUNCH IN THIS AREA. YOU DON'T NEED TO TAKE THEM A CUP OF COFFEE. ALL YOU DO IS GO IN EVERY COUPLE OF WEEKS, HAND A BROCHURE TO EVERY BREATHING SOUL IN THE PLACE AND LEAVE. USUALLY, AT LEAST ONE PERSON WILL STOP YOU AND ASK ABOUT LIFE INSURANCE. DON'T HAND ONE TO THE CUSTOMERS— THAT MAKES THEM MAD. THEY THINK THEY HAVE BEEN LEFT OUT OF THE BUSINESS EQUATION, ANYWAY, SO WHEN YOU SHOW THEM THE LEAST BIT OF ATTENTION, THEY RESPOND.

Savings and loan, and bank loan officers are a tremendous source of new clients.

BETWEEN 1990 AND THE YEAR 2000, NOT ONE WEEK EVER WENT BY, 52 WEEKS OUT OF THE YEAR, THAT WE DIDN'T GET AT LEAST ONE CALL FROM A LOAN OFFICER SAYING, "COULD YOU RUN OVER TO THE C & S BRANCH BANK AT THE CORNER OF BUFORD HIGHWAY AND DEKALB ROAD? WE HAVE A CLIENT HERE NEEDING TO

BUY LIFE INSURANCE AND WE DON'T WANT TO MAKE THE LOAN UNTIL WE ARE SURE HE IS INSURABLE."

NOT ONE WEEK DID WE GO WITHOUT A SALE. THE BEST PART IS, NOT ONE INSURANCE AGENT IN HISTORY HAS EVER GONE BY AND ASKED THEM FOR THEIR BUSINESS. YOU ARE THE ONLY ONE.

Eighteen

A Challenge

Anyone who reads my book and listens to my CDs and tells me that my program doesn't work, well, here is what I will do: I will come to any city in the United States with a population of 50,000 or more. I will take 500 of my brochures and start walking.

No car. No pocket money. Rain or shine. At the end of an 8-hour day, I will make in first-year commissions a minimum of $1,000 and if I don't, then I will pay you $10,000. Guaranteed.

THIS IS A VIABLE OFFER TO ANYONE READING THIS. However, if I do make that $1,000, then you pay me the $10,000. This is a fair offer, and if this doesn't absolutely prove that I believe in what I do, and that my bird dog program and my "Affordable Life Brochure" work, then you should change occupations.

Nineteen

SBA Loan Originators

The United States government requires that every SBA loan they give or guarantee be covered with life insurance. Anyone applying for and receiving a loan must buy life insurance, and not only that, they must pay an annual premium before the loan check is given to them.

There are two programs. With one program the money comes directly from the government, and with the second, called the 7A program, a bank loans the money and the SBA just guarantees a large portion of it

These loans average approximately $500,000 and can be quite lucrative for the insurance agent writing the coverage. The policy must be for the term of the loan, meaning if it's a twenty-year loan, then the policy must be a twenty-year-level term policy. The average age of the person getting these loans is over 50. This being said, this is one of the most lucrative opportunities for an agent seeking to write this type coverage.

Business owners can go directly to a bank to apply for a loan, but then he or she must find a CPA to do the loan package and take him or her through the process. Banks usually have no clue as to how to package a loan and most CPAs don't either. This is why most people either go, or are referred by a bank, to a SBA loan origination company. There is only a handful in most states, but it only takes one of them to make someone a great deal of money.

Loan originators are frustrated with almost every loan because life insurance is the one thing they usually forget about until the last minute, and then they can't place the loan until the coverage is in force. That's when they find out the man applying for the loan has severe health problems, making it difficult, at best, to get coverage. This is great for us because the premium is usually quadrupled, at the least.

Remember, the applicant must buy the life insurance. He has to pay whatever the cost is, and the premium is taken out of the loan proceeds as an annual premium. Once, I wrote a case for $700,000 on a man who had recently had cancer surgery. First Standard Financial was the loan origination firm that sent the case to me. I got it issued, but the premium was $23,000 yearly. I don't have to tell you that the client was quite upset, but he had no choice but to take the policy and pay the annual premium. What a great way to make a living.

Call the SBA office in your state and they will have a list of all the loan originators in their state.

HOW DO YOU APPROACH AN SBA LOAN ORIGINATION COMPANY?

You set up an appointment. It will be difficult to get past the main assistant to the owner. You tell her that you are an area manager with a major life insurance company. You are looking for an SBA loan origination company because you have clients who are looking for a business loan or quite possibly, an SBA guaranteed loan and you are interviewing firms that might want to apply to you for the business. THAT GETS YOU IN THE DOOR.

Proceed with your standard presentation, emphasizing the blocks that a potential client can check asking for a business or SBA loan, and tell the man that, if you get life insurance referrals, you will send them a fair share of the leads that come in.

They are not allowed to require someone to buy from you, but 100% of the time, the people who are applying for the loan will buy from you.

THAT IS IT. I PERSONALLY AVERAGED ABOUT $200,000 IN FIRST-YEAR COMMISSIONS FROM JUST ONE SBA LOAN ORIGINATION COMPANY FOR OVER TEN YEARS IN ATLANTA, GEORGIA. GO SEEK THEM OUT.

DO NOT PAY A FINDER'S FEE. YOUR APPROACH IS THIS: WE WILL HELP YOU. WE WILL SEND YOU POTENTIAL CLIENTS, IF YOU DO THE SAME FOR ME. THEY WILL HAVE LOANS RIGHT THEN FOR YOU TO CALL THE PEOPLE, THAT DAY. THEY WANT YOU TO WRITE THE INSURANCE SO THEY DON'T HAVE TO WORRY ABOUT IT. YOU DON'T HAVE TO PAY THEM ANYTHING.

REFER THEM BUSINESS, WHICH WE WILL DO. SBA LOAN ORIGINATORS ARE A GREAT SOURCE OF INCOME AND ARE GREAT LIFE INSURANCE BIRD DOGS. THERE ARE NOT MANY OF THEM, BUT THEY ARE A FABULOUS SOURCE OF NEW CLIENTS.

REMEMBER, THEY WILL TELL YOU THAT THEY ARE NOT ALLOWED TO SELL LIFE INSURANCE OR THAT THEY ALREADY HAVE SOMEONE TO SEND THE BUSINESS TO. THIS IS OK. JUST LEAVE SOME BROCHURES. HAND ONE OR MORE TO EVERYONE IN THE PLACE.TALK TO ALL EXECUTIVES AND CLERICAL HELP IN THE PLACE. SOMETIMES WE GOT MORE BUSINESS OUT OF THE SECRETARY THAN WE DID THE LOAN OFFICER, AND IN FACT, MOST OF THE TIME, IT CAME FROM THE CLERICAL HELP. IF YOU GO BACK ONCE A MONTH TO SAY HELLO, THEY WILL APPRECIATE YOUR PERSISTENCE AND WILL CALL YOU. I KNOW, BECAUSE I DID IT FOR YEARS.

CHAPTER Twenty

Are You Beginning a New Career?

A young man interviewed and took a job with Mutual of New York in their Atlanta office some years back. He spent the better part of the first three months in class, studying everything from products to estate planning. He was a true expert in the field of life insurance.

Well, the day came. He goes into the general agent's office one bright, shiny Monday morning and gets a handshake and the words, "Go get 'em, tiger. We think you are a real up-and-comer." On Thursday, he arrives early at the office in Atlanta, and after waiting a few minutes, is summoned into the general agent's office. "How did you do?" he asks.

"Well, not too bad. On Monday, I drove to Savannah and sold an elderly gentleman a $10,000 whole life policy. On Tuesday, I didn't sell anything, and on Wednesday, the man in Savannah called and decided to cancel saying he decided he didn't want the policy, after all. SO, I GUESS, TUESDAY WAS MY BEST DAY!"

Well, this, or something similar, is what usually happens to most new agents in the business. That is why 9 in 10 agents entering the life insurance business won't last through the third year.

It isn't because of his knowledge of the business. It isn't because he has a bad company or his commission isn't enough. It isn't because his company has not planned and priced good products for him to sell. It is because he does not know how to promote himself. He does not know how to get in front of people who want to buy life insurance. He doesn't know how, so he drives up and down the highway, not knowing what to do. This is what my bird dog marketing program does. It gives this man, new to the business, a place to go, a person to sell to.

Most everyone reading this, right now gets up every day of their lives unemployed. That's right, without a job. Working on a commission basis only is not a job. It is a direction, but not a job. If you don't sell something on any given day, regardless of how many telephone calls you make, how many letters you write and mail, or how many people you see, if you don't sell something, you are unemployed because you did not make any money.

No one really ever understands what we all have to go through, the mental anguish we all suffer most of the time. So, change things. Get employed, and the only way to get employed is to find a way to get in front of people who want to buy from you. And you know there is this person the minute you wake up in the morning. You know you will sell something that day, so that second you open your eyes, you have a job, and the bird dog program will do that for you.

Twenty-one

Stockbrokers

THIS IS ONE OF THE SHORTEST CHAPTERS OF THE BOOK, AND FRANKLY, I STILL THINK I AM SPENDING TOO MUCH TIME ON THESE BARRACUDAS, BUT HERE GOES.

Stockbrokers, on the whole, are what we call, down South, horses' asses.

They tend to be very condescending toward insurance agents. However, if you approach them correctly, they will send you high end, more affluent customers. The problem today is that probably half of them are out of work, and it will be some time before they have another job in their field, if ever, and if the arrogance and hubris of the ones I know carries through to most other stockbrokers, then all that happens to them is justified.

In the meantime, you can find many of them greeting people at Wal-Mart, and as far as I am concerned, those arrogant, selfish crooks should be digging ditches. If there is anyone reading this who doesn't know by now that I don't care for most stockbrokers, then keep reading.

Now, if you use the standard approach, show them a sample application request card where there is a place for people to check if they want a stockbroker. Convince them you will be sending them new customers, and you will get a smattering of business in the future.

SOLICIT STOCKBROKERS. THEY CAN BE A SOURCE OF HIGHER END CLIENTS. JUST DON'T KILL YOURSELF GOING UP STAIRS TO SEE THEM, BECAUSE YOU MIGHT GET HIT BY SEVERAL OF THEM ON THE WAY DOWN.

CHAPTER Twenty-two

Critique

As this book of mine comes to an end, remember this, if you don't remember anything else: STOP BLAMING OTHERS FOR YOUR MISTAKES OR FAILURES. TAKE RESPONSIBILITY FOR YOUR FUTURE LIKE I DID MANY YEARS AGO. I AM NO DIFFERENT FROM YOU, EXCEPT I PROBABLY AM NOT NEARLY AS GOOD A SALESMAN AS YOU ARE, AND THAT IS YOUR JOB— NOTHING ELSE. YOU SELL. YES, YOU ARE A GREAT SALESPERSON. BUT THAT HAS ABSOLUTELY NOTHING TO DO WITH SUCCESS.

MOST ALL OF US ARE GREAT SALESMEN. THE SUCCESSFUL AGENT KNOWS ONE THING THAT MOST OTHER AGENTS DO NOT AND THAT IS HOW TO GET IN FRONT OF PEOPLE WHO WANT TO BUY LIFE INSURANCE, ON A REGULAR BASIS, WITHOUT HAVING TO COLD CALL. THAT'S IT. HOWEVER, YOU MUST DO IT FOR YOURSELF. NO ONE ELSE WILL HELP, BECAUSE THEY DON'T KNOW HOW TO FIND PEOPLE TO BUY LIFE INSURANCE, SO HOW CAN THEY TEACH YOU?

CHAPTER Twenty-three

Real Estate Agencies

THIS IS ANOTHER SHORT CHAPTER, BECAUSE MOST OF WHAT I NEED TO COVER HAS ALREADY BEEN COVERED A HALF DOZEN TIMES.

Like stockbrokers, you can find a certain degree of hubris with many real estate agents, but nowhere near that of a stockbroker. They can be the most difficult bird dog to set up, but also the easiest, if you know how. And guess what? I know how.

First: You set up an appointment. You do this the same way as most all the others. You call, say that many of your clients, on occasion, ask for a referral to a real estate agent, and that is why you are calling.

Follow the same course. Set up an appointment, and the great things is, when you get that appointment and finish your presentation, ask to see other agents. They will usually do it—I don't know why, because they are all so competitive. The most ruthless people I have ever encountered in forty years as a businessman are florists and real estate agents, most all women.

Second: You make the presentation. You do this the same way as most others, except, DO NOT OFFER THEM ANY FEE FOR A

REFERRED CLIENT. IT MAKES THEM MAD, AND LIKE ANYONE WHO MAKES THEIR LIVING IN LARGE SUMS INSTEAD OF SMALL, WEEKLY SUMS LIKE THE REST OF US DO, FIFTY BUCKS IS MORE OF AN INSULT THAN ANYTHING. PERSONALLY, I WOULD THINK THEY WOULD JUMP AT ANYTHING, SINCE SO FEW OF THEM ARE SELLING ANYTHING IN TODAY'S TIMES. STILL, BEST NOT TO OFFER.

Third: You are finished. You called. You set up the appointment. You went to see the agent. You made your presentation. You handed out brochures to everyone in the place. You left.

Service, of course, but just a quick stop-by, on occasion, is plenty. If you can ever, ever refer to them someone looking to buy or sell a house, they will send you business from that day on, but usually you have to start the process with real estate agents. You must send them someone first, before they will ever send you a potential client. I do not know why, but it is usually this way.

Twenty-four

Summary

THIS IS MORE OF A SUMMARY OF ALL OUR CHAPTERS. I WANT TO STRESS THAT THE ACTUAL TELEPHONE APPOINTMENT SETTING, THE ACTUAL PRE-SENTATION, AND SERVICE WORK IS VERY SIMILAR, IF NOT IDENTICAL, REGARDLESS OF THE TYPE OF BIRD DOG YOU ARE ATTEMPTING TO SET UP. STUDY. MEMORIZE. IF YOU DO IT THE WAY I TELL YOU TO DO IT, IT WILL WORK.

I HAVE HAD A PROBLEM WITH TWO WORDS FOR MANY YEARS. SUDDENLY, ABOUT THE TIME I TURNED AGE FORTY, PEOPLE STOPPED HAVING "PROBLEMS." NOW THEY ARE "CHALLENGES," NO LONGER PROBLEMS. THE WORLD IS FREE OF PROBLEMS. SOMEONE DYING OF CANCER, WITH THREE DAYS TO LIVE: NOT A PROBLEM, THEY JUST HAVE A CHALLENGE TO LIVE FOUR DAYS. I STILL HAVE PROBLEMS THAT I WANT TO SOLVE. YOU CAN HAVE ALL THE CHALLENGES YOU WANT. THE OTHER WORD IS "TELL." I DON'T TELL ANYONE ANYTHING ANY LONGER. I CAN'T TELL MY DOG TO GO FETCH THE BONE. I CAN ONLY "SHARE," NOT TELL, BUT SHARE. NOW I HAVE TO SHARE WITH MY DOG THE INFORMATION NECESSARY FOR HIM TO GO FETCH THE BONE.

I AM TELLING YOU ABOUT THESE TWO WORDS FOR THIS REASON: I AM TELLING YOU WHAT TO DO IN THIS BOOK. I'M NOT CHALLENGING YOU. YOU EITHER DO IT, OR YOU DON'T.

CHAPTER Twenty-five

Script for the Bird Dog Presentation

1 *"Mr./Ms._____, my name is _____, and I am an area representative for Mutual of Omaha. We spoke briefly yesterday. Am I on time?"*

Then you start walking to his office. The reason you use Mutual of Omaha is that people recognize the name. They have credibility as a strong company, are financially sound, and there is a one-in-four chance, either they or a family member has a policy with them. We do represent Mutual of Omaha, and the policy we sell may just be one for them.

YOU HAND THAT PERSON A BROCHURE AND HAND A BROCHURE TO EVERYONE WITHIN A REASONABLE DISTANCE TO YOU. INCLUDE EVERY EMPLOYEE YOU SEE, BECAUSE THE BROCHURE IS THE KEY TO EVERYTHING. UNLESS YOU HAND THAT PERSON A BROCHURE, YOU MIGHT AS WELL LEAVE RIGHT THEN.

THE BROCHURE IS KEY TO EVERYTHING.

The blank line on the brochure is for you to fill in the type of business they are. If it's a bank loan officer, you say BANK. If it's a mortgage loan officer you say MORTGAGE BANKER, and so on. The reason you walk to their office is because, if you try to pitch them while they are standing in the outer office, it is too easy for them to say no. They try to impress the other employees with their resistance to anyone wanting anything from them.

They try to impress their employees by saying no. You will never sign up a bird dog in the outer office.

2 *"Mr. / Ms. _____. What we do is simple. If you identify a person who expresses a desire to buy life insurance or if you have a client to whom you recommend the purchase of life insurance and they express an interest....send them to us and we will do all the work. We will complete the application, order the exams, arrange for a blood draw if necessary. We will contact the doctors' offices, we will do everything. You do nothing but give us the referral by filling out one of these cards. Fax to us and then we pay you a commission based on this schedule."*

All you are doing, all you are saying is send me some people who want to buy life insurance, and we will pay you a commission. Remember: there is a $50 max commission you can pay anyone who is not a licensed life insurance agent. All but three states allow you to pay a $50 finder's fee/facilitator's fee if they are not licensed. The chart of different commissions is for licensed people only.

THEN YOU HAND HIM THE CHART THAT BREAKS DOWN THE COMMISSIONS FOR THE DIFFERENT PRODUCTS WE SELL. THIS CHART APPLIES TO REAL ESTATE AGENTS, MORTGAGE BROKERS, INDEPENDENT PROPERTY AND CASUALTY INSURANCE AGENCIES, BANK LOAN OFFICERS, SAVINGS AND LOAN OFFICERS, BOOKKEEPERS CPAs, STOCKBROKERS, HEALTH INSURANCE SALESMEN, AND TAX PREPARATION OFFICES.

3

**TERM LIFE INSURANCE $50. THIS EQUATES TO $25 TO BUSINESS / $25 TO PERSON. CASH VALUE LIFE INSURANCE 25% OF THE COMMISSION WITH $100 MINIMUM. $50 GOES TO THE PERSON REFERRING THE NEW CLIENT. THE REMAINDER GOES TO THE BUSINESS.

**Based on a 95% commission schedule
(Average nationwide is $345.55)

DISABILITY INCOME INSURANCE: 30%

> *OF THE COMMISSION, WITH A $75 MINIMUM.*

(Average nationwide is $300.50)

IRA AND 401K: 30%

> *OF THE COMMISSION, WITH $125 MINIMUM.*

(Average nationwide commission to agency is $556.75)

ANNUITIES: 25%

> *OF THE COMMISSION, WITH $750 MINIMUM.*

(Average nationwide is $2,350)

ANY OTHER PRODUCT SALES NEGOTIATED.

4

> *"Mr. / Ms._____, most of our clients we obtain through our national advertising are self-employed people. They are small business owners. We distribute tens of millions of the brochures you have in your hand right now, nationwide, with a great many going right here to your state, and if you will look on the Application Return Card, you will see some boxes next to*

questions, and some of those questions pertain to your business. We will be more than happy, in addition to the above fee schedule, to send you any leads we get from our national advertising to you. You send us some business, we will send you business. It is as simple as that."

NOW COMES THE KEY STATEMENT FOR YOU. SAY THIS CORRECTLY, AND YOU HAVE JUST SET UP A NEW BIRD DOG.

5   *"Mr. / Ms. _____, before we go on, I need you to take a minute and have you tell me about yourself and your business, what exactly it is you do. This is a two-way street, as I'm sure you know. Tell me about yourself. Just as you must be concerned about who Mutual of Omaha is, we must know the same about you before we send our clients to your office."*

IT IS VITAL TO SAY MUTUAL OF OMAHA IN ABOVE SENTENCE AND NOT YOUR NAME. IF YOU SAY YOUR NAME, IT WILL PUT A SEED OF DOUBT IN HIS MIND ABOUT WHETHER YOU ARE REALLY CREDIBLE OR NOT, BUT IF YOU SAY MUTUAL OF OMAHA, HE KNOWS WHO THEY ARE AND IT WILL ELIMINATE THAT CONCERN. THIS IS VERY IMPORTANT, BUT EVERYTHING I AM TELLING YOU IS TRUE, THIS PERSON WILL TALK FOR ONE MINUTE, OR ONE HOUR, IF YOU LET THEM. THEY PROBABLY LOVE THE SOUND OF THEIR OWN VOICE SO MUCH THEY WILL TALK FOREVER. PEOPLE LOVE TO TALK ABOUT THEMSELVES. RARELY DO THEY HAVE ANYONE WHO ASKS THIS. THAT PERSON SEES IN YOU SOMEONE WHO REALLY CARES, AND YOU SHOULD CARE ABOUT THAT PERSON, BECAUSE

YOUR INCOME WILL BE DEPENDENT IN PART ON HIM OR HER IN THE FUTURE.

Now, it's time for the assumed close, and it is a little different, depending on the type business you are in. A close for a bank officer is a little different from a close on a property and casualty insurance agency, so here are the differences.

For mortgage brokers, bank loan officers, bookkeepers, CPAs, stockbrokers, health insurance salesmen, SBA loan originators and savings and loan officers, it's easy, because you are only dealing with one person.

You are not getting permission from them for others to give out brochures for you, so your close is simple:

6

"Mr./ Ms. _____, thank you for your time. Let me give you a few brochures. You can keep them on the corner of your desk...or I have this little paper take-one box you can put some in, whatever is convenient for you. If you want a reminder, here is a little card that you can put in a convenient place to remind you to ask your customers to buy life insurance, whatever is easiest for you."

THE CARD YOU GIVE THEM IS NOT SO IMPORTANT HERE WITH THESE BIRD DOGS AS IT IS WITH THE PROPERTY AND CASUALTY AGENTS, BUT IF THEY WILL USE IT, THEN GET THEM TO TAPE IT TO THE SURFACE OF THEIR DESK. CHOOSE A PLACE WHERE THEY WILL SEE IT OFTEN

·_____

(Red, White and Blue)

"Picture of American Flag"

$10,000 OR MORE, EVERY YEAR,

POSSIBLE FOR LIFE INSURANCE REFERRALS.

This is it. Just the above.

_____

Now we are finished with everything but property and casualty insurance agencies.

FOR CAPTIVE AGENCIES, LIKE FARMERS, COTTON STATES, ALLSTATE, ETC., (FORGET STATE FARM—YOU ARE WASTING YOUR TIME) YOU WILL SAY THIS INSTEAD OF (3) ABOVE.

"Mr./Ms. _____*, we work with* _____ *agencies and agents across the country in writing life insurance policies on people who don't normally qualify for your standard underwriting. We are very aggressive with diabetes, heart problems, etc."*

WHEN YOU APPROACH A CAPTIVE PROPERTY AND CASUALTY INSURANCE AGENCY, YOU MUST GO IN AS A SUB-STANDARD BROKER, WITH YOUR ONLY INTENTION BEING THAT YOU WANT TO SELL LIFE INSURANCE TO THEIR CLIENTS WHO DON'T QUALIFY FOR A LIFE INSURANCE POLICY WITH THEIR COMPANY. ANY OTHER PRESENTATION OR IDEA WON'T FLY. IN THE WEST, FARMERS AGENTS ARE PARTICULARLY EASY TO SET UP THIS WAY.

You ask them to farm out life business that they can't write, and we do a great deal of it for agents. THEN, WHEN YOU GET TO #4, YOU EMPHASIZE THAT THE BOX TO THE LEFT THAT SAYS ANNUITIES PERTAINS TO THEM, AND YOU SAY,

"Mr./Ms. _____, do you sell annuities? We do get requests for annuities, on occasion, and would be glad to refer them to you."

ALL THESE AGENTS ARE PRESSURED TO WRITE ANNUITIES. THERE ISN'T A MEETING THEY ATTEND THAT THEY ARE NOT PRESSURED AND PUSHED TO WRITE ANNUITIES, AND IF THERE IS A HOPE THAT YOU MIGHT SEND THEM JUST ONE, YOU HAVE A BIRD DOG.

FOR NON-CAPTIVE PROPERTY AND CASUALTY AGENTS, YOU GIVE THE PRESENTATION EXACTLY AS IT IS ABOVE AND YOUR CLOSE IS THE SAME. HOWEVER, YOU ADD THIS:

"Well, Mr. / Ms. _____, all I have to do is hand out a few brochures to your employees up front. Would you like a poster or two in your office? Then, you spend a few minutes with the people in the front office training them on what to say to clients who come into the office, clients who call the office, the type of client you are looking for, etc. That is it."

Now, you have set up a bird dog, maybe dozens of them. If you service them correctly, you'll have a business for the first time in your life.

BELOW IS A SUMMARY OF THE PRESENTATION. MEMORIZE IT. ONE IN TEN WILL MEMORIZE IT AND THAT IS THE ONE WHO MAKES ALL THE MONEY.

"Mr./Ms._____, my name is _____, and I am an area representative for Mutual of Omaha. Mutual of Omaha works with a great many _____ across the state. Would you give me two

minutes of your time to share with you how we need your help, Mr. / Ms. _____? What we do is simple. If you identify a person who expresses a desire to buy life insurance, we will do all the work and pay you a commission. We will write the application, order the exams, contact the doctor's offices for reports— everything. We will do it all. All you do is send us someone who has said they want to buy life insurance.

"Here is our chart showing the commission ranges we say to you, and even a little to your employees out front, as a bonus or raise, that doesn't come out of your pocket.

"In addition, Mr. / Ms._____, what we need your help on is our referrals. If you will note on the left side of the Application Request Card you have, there are a number of boxes our clients can check to show that they are interested in other products, and one of them is _____. You help us, and we help you. Through our national advertising in MasterCard and Visa bills, we get a great many requests from individuals requesting what you sell and we would appreciate an opportunity to form a relationship with you whereby you send us anyone looking to buy life insurance and we send you anyone who comes to us for life insurance but also wants to buy what you sell.

"Now, Mr./Ms. _____, before we really know if we can help each other, I need to know a little more about you and what you do here, what your business is looking for.

"Well, that's about it. Here are some brochures. Keep them in your desk or keep them in these take-one boxes. Here is a poster, and now I will take a minute or two with your people out here. I look forward to doing business with you."

MEMORIZE THIS AND YOU WILL BE SUCCESSFUL.

Twenty-six

Research

I do thank you for taking the time to read this book. If you want to be that one-in-ten, read it again and again and again, and every time you read it, you will find something new. Again, I want to thank the brokers who contributed so much to what has been said.

Tonight, I want you to research. Start with health insurance agents and then go to each category. Pick out the top twenty you find in each group. Get a three-ring binder and make sections, just like you did in high school. Don't sit there and set up folders and spread sheets on your computer. For goodness sake, throw that computer out the window for a day. Now, start calling. Set up at least five appointments for tomorrow and the day after tomorrow. The first day, see five health insurance agents. The second day, see five mortgage brokers.

You will get to the other categories in a day or two. Go meet the people. Do exactly what I told you to do in this book. Remember, the brochure is king. Hand one to everyone you see. Make your short, one-minute presentation, exactly as I wrote it. Have it memorized. Some people would recommend to you that you change it so it fits your style better, but I am telling you that you should forget your style, it has never worked, and then memorize and say your presentation exactly like I say.

You should set up anywhere between two and ten appointments. Chances are you will set up the smaller amount until your jitters are gone. You will be nervous, initially. You will lose your chance to set up one or more bird dogs because you stumble in your presentation, but expect that.

Don't get to the end of the day and quit because you are not as successful as you think you should be. What we do works and has worked for over two decades. The important thing is that when you do get the OK to proceed from a new bird dog, don't hurry and forget to do the most important thing.

Spend time with your bird dogs and train them on what to say and why the brochure works.

Teach them how to fill out the application request form attached to the brochure and stress that their finder's fee only comes from application request cards that they, not the prospect, fill out. You burn into their head, their memory, that you are their new life insurance agent. You briefly go over all the products you sell, from life insurance to annuities, and you know what? One in three will buy a life insurance policy from you right on the spot.

OK, Mr./Ms. Life Insurance Broker, get up and go. Hang up the telephone and start talking face-to-face. Forget the past; forget the people who have been rude to you; forget your failures, and get going. My good friend, Les Turner, in Knoxville, Tennessee, told me that his first full day handing out brochures, he asked more people to buy life insurance from him than he had in his thirty-year career. He told me he made new friends and had enough appointments to last him a week. He was so very excited. He had a new life after that. You can too.

JUST GET UP OFF OF YOUR REAR END AND GO OUT INTO THE WORLD. THE BIRD DOG PROGRAM WILL CHANGE YOUR LIFE.

P. S. I would love to further discuss your career with our agency. Just call me. I take and/or return all calls. 877 250 442   8

Twenty-seven

Build An Agency The Right Way

There are actually two sales when doing the Bird Dog Program. One sale is to the bird dog himself and the other sale is the sale of the life insurance to the person whom the bird dog has sent you. Two sales, and you know what I have found frequently, and one of the reasons some of the brokers who come to me don't succeed? I've found that many good men can't make both sales. They can set up and service new bird dogs but they can't complete the cycle and make that life insurance sale, or they are lousy at setting up bird dogs, but are great at setting up an appointment and making the life insurance sale.

Therefore, we are finding that the best way to pursue the bird dog program is using a TEAM APPROACH, WITH ONE BROKER SETTING UP AND SERVICING THE BIRD DOGS, AND THE SECOND AGENT COMPLETING THE PROCESS AND MAKING THE ACTUAL SALE.

The person who sets up and services the bird dogs does not have to be licensed, but can be. That person is not selling insurance. They are simply setting up relationships, strategic relationships, that will generate leads. This is the most difficult position to fill. It should be a professional. It should be someone with a good appearance, a good personality, and especially, a drive to succeed. This person can be an agent, but usually we find, with the economy the way it is, that there is no shortage of people qualified for the job. How do you find one? Simply put an ad in the newspaper:

40-year-old company

expanding and putting in

client set-up and

maintenance positions.

Call to apply.

That's really it. You should get quite a few responses, but again, you want a mature person with drive and enthusiasm, who will work for a rate of per-lead-generated or overall percentage of profits, not of commission generated, but of profits to the business. You can pay a salary if you want, but chances are, you don't have the money to pay anyone a salary right now. It will be more difficult to find someone for this position, but not impossible. If you hire an insurance agent for this job, and that is always a possibility, then that person is used to working on a commission and you have no problem.

BY NOW YOU SHOULD HAVE REALIZED THAT YOU SHOULD BE THE PERSON WHO SETS UP THE BIRD DOGS. YOU DO NOT HIRE SOMEONE TO DO THAT. YOU HIRE THE AGENTS TO MAKE THE SALES, BUT YOU DO THE FRONT-END WORK. IF YOU DON'T WANT TO, THEN YOU HIRE SOMEONE. BUT IF YOU FIND YOU CAN'T SET UP BIRD DOGS PROPERLY, THEN YOU SHOULD SERIOUSLY CONSIDER BECOMING AN AGENT AGAIN, AND SELL AND WORK FOR SOMEONE ELSE.

Now, you hire the agent, and for us, that is easy. Our brokers have the backup of me. We just turn on our voice broadcast machine and call every licensed agent in any zip code, deliver a message saying we are looking for agents to work our leads in this area, and you won't have but ten thousand agents apply. That is it.

So, you have hired a person (OR YOU MADE THE RIGHT DECISION TO DO IT YOURSELF) to set up relationships with bird dogs and you have hired one agent which may be expanded to two agents depending on how good a job your number-one person does. Then you hire another, then another, until you have reached a point where you can keep the number of agents you have busy. Then it is time to hire a person to find bird dogs for you in another geographical area.

Now you establish a territory, and my suggestion is to take your zip code and expand out until you get a population base of 500,000, rural areas less. This will give you plenty of room to set up all the bird dogs you will ever want or need and leave room for expansion in the future.

REMEMBER, 90% OF ALL SALES YOU WILL PROBABLY EVER MAKE ARE WITHIN A 100 MILE RADIUS OF YOUR HOME. YOU DO NOT NEED TO HIRE SOMEONE A THOUSAND MILES AWAY TO BUILD AN AGENCY. IT IS RIGHT IN YOUR BACKYARD. THERE IS AN OLD SAYING THAT YOU WILL DRIVE BY MORE BUSINESS THAN YOU WILL EVER WRITE, AND YOU WILL.

So, you have hired a person (OR MADE THE DECISION TO DO IT YOURSELF) for position number #1, and an agent for position number #2, and you have established your territory. Once you have your first territory up and running, you will then set up a second territory. You will do so with two people just like before, but we will talk about expansion another day.

Right now, all you should be concerned with is getting one territory set up. The compensation you should pay these two people should not exceed 60% of the first year's premium. You should not pay more than this. You do not have to pay more than this. Assuming you are on a 100% contract, this leaves you 40% and that is a respectable override. You will be working quite hard. You will be helping set up those "bird dog" relationships. You will be setting appointments and making sales when your agents are sick or have quit.

You are not going home to sit in your easy chair and watch television. You must get compensated for your work and your ideas. This book you are reading right now took decades to perfect and you might as well take advantage of it.

The duties of the agent are to make it to the appointment on time and make the sale. They should have two appointments, minimum, daily, for four days a week. That is it. If they do their job, they should make a minimum of six sales a week for a minimum annual premium of $6000.

Of that 60%, the agent will get 40%. So, if he works approximately 6 hours daily, 4 days a week, 40 weeks a year, a six-figure income will be created. I promise you that, regardless of what an agent will tell you, he does not make six figures.

Now, the person you have hired to set up the bird dogs (OR YOU) will get compensation equivalent to 20% of the first-year premium. (IF IT IS YOU, THEN YOUR OVERRIDE IS INCREASED TO A MINIMUM OF 60%).

However, they get this 20% for each agent they set up leads for, and it is possible for one person to set up enough bird dogs to generate enough appointments for four agents. It happens every day. If that is the case, this person is the highest income person but they certainly earn it.

It is the responsibility of the person who sets up the bird dog relationships to do this:

A. Set up the relationships.

B. Service the relationships.

C. Send out the weekly newsletter.

D. Set the appointments for the agents.

*A above...*well, that is what this entire book is about...how to set up the relationships. No need to expand on that here.

*B above...*SERVICE IS KING. EVERY WEEK YOU MUST MAKE CONTACT, AND PREFERABLY THAT CONTACT IS A PERSONAL VISIT. BIRTHDAY CARDS, A GIFT AS SMALL AS A CUP OF COFFEE ARE APPRECIATED. SERVICE THAT ACCOUNT AND YOU WILL HAVE AN ACCOUNT FOREVER.

*C above...*THE MOST IMPORTANT THING TO SERVICING THE BIRD DOG ACCOUNTS IS A WEEKLY NEWSLETTER TO EACH BIRD DOG TELLING THEM WHAT OTHERS ARE DOING, SUCH AS, SALLY SUE BROWN AT THE SMITH AGENCY IN TALLADEGA, ALABAMA, GOT A CHECK THIS WEEK FOR $250 FOR THE NEW CLIENTS SHE SENT HER PERSON FROM THE AMERICAN INSURANCE INSTITUTE. WHAT A GREAT WEEK FOR SALLY SUE!

Just four or five of these little blurbs each week will make the difference in what you do. These people should be treated and constantly reinforced and motivated just like an agency field force of salesmen. Do this and you have a bird dog forever. Don't do this and you won't keep a bird dog for more than a month.

*D above...*seems a little time consuming but the person who sets up and services the bird dogs must also process the leads and set the appointments for each of that person's agents; 2 appointments daily, 4 days a week, per agent. If that person sets and services a bird dog correctly, then it's very possible to generate enough leads for 4 agents, full time and that is where the big money is made. If just half the policies are written with IAP life, then you can double your commission, as they pay the same commission in the second year as they do the first. DID YOU READ THIS CORRECTLY? IAP LIFE PAYS THE FIRST-YEAR COMMISSION TWICE. IT'S LIKE WRITING TWO POLICIES EVERY TIME YOU WRITE ONE. THIS COMPANY PAYS THE HIGHEST COMMISSION, BY FAR, THAT I HAVE SEEN IN MY 41-YEAR CAREER IN THIS BUSINESS. JUST ONE POLICY FOR $100 MONTHLY

PREMIUM WILL BRING YOU, THE AGENT, A MINIMUM OF $2000 COMMISSION. IT'S THE TRUTH.

Unless the person who sets up the bird dogs also sets up the appointments for the agent, you will never get an agent to work on 40% commission.

However, if you do generate the lead and you set the appointment, you will have agents fighting over the position you have to offer them.

Let's move on. The solicitor and the agent must be kept apart. It's best if they don't even know each other. Why? Because, within the first two weeks, you will have the agent going to the solicitor and saying, "Well, what do we need Joe Agent for? You just set up the bird dogs and I will go sell them and we keep everything."

IF YOU DON'T THINK THIS WILL HAPPEN, THEN YOU SET UP YOUR BUSINESS WITH THE SOLICITOR AND THE AGENT BECOMING BIG BUDDIES. IF YOU ARE THE SOLICITOR, THEN YOU DON'T HAVE TO WORRY ABOUT THIS EITHER.

Also, you must get an agreement signed by all solicitors and agents saying they will not copy your materials, saying that if it does come to a lawsuit between them and you for any purpose, that the courts in your home county will oversee the process, otherwise you will have to hire a lawyer in a city hundreds, even thousands, of miles away to sue someone. There are other clauses, but I can go over that with you another time.

The American Insurance Institute will maintain solicitors on a national basis to help all brokers doing our program. They will come in and make calls with you, offer training, and be there for you whenever necessary.

Summary: Hire one solicitor to set up and service the bird dogs— BUT IT'S A THOUSAND TIMES BETTER IF YOU DO IT YOURSELF. Hire 1–2 agents per solicitor to make the actual life insurance sale. Keep them apart. Don't pay more than 60%

compensation. You oversee the entire thing and make sure it runs like a well-oiled machine, and if you do, it will.

Thanks for taking the time to read our book. Follow what was written and it will change your life for the better in the future. If you are one of those 20% who have the fire in their spirit to get up and do something, then this might be what you have been looking for.

I hope to hear from you.

W. RANDY MURRAY

WWW.THEAMERICANINSURANCEINSTITUTE.COM

RMURRAY@WINDSTREAM.NET

www.ingramcontent.com/pod-product-compliance
Lightning Source LLC
Chambersburg PA
CBHW051921170526
45168CB00001B/487